The PETE ROSE Story

The PETE ROSE Story

AN AUTOBIOGRAPHY

INTRODUCTION BY JOE GARAGIOLA

THE WORLD PUBLISHING COMPANY
New York and Cleveland

Published by the World Publishing Company

2231 West 110th Street, Cleveland, Ohio 44102

Published simultaneously in Canada by

Nelson, Foster & Scott Ltd.

First Printing—1970

Library of Congress Catalog Card Number: 71-120126

Printed in the United States of America

WORLD PUBLISHING
TIMES MIRROR

Dedicated to all the people—managers,
players, fans, news writers, and broadcasters
—who have gone out of their way
to make me look better than I am;
and to my dad, who made everything happen.

INTRODUCTION BY JOE GARAGIOLA

There are some pictures that are just impossible for the mind to imagine. For example, can you picture Tiny Tim as an umpire? Or Zsa Zsa Gabor as a librarian? I'll give you a real tough one. Try to imagine Pete Rose as a senior citizen, sitting quietly in the sun, and dozing off in the middle of a conversation. No way.

It's more likely that when he's ninety, Pete Rose will probably be coaching a Little League team. Not only that, but instead of telling kids why they should run to first base when they get a walk, he'll be demonstrating it to them.

One reason that it's so tough to imagine Pete Rose as an old man is that he never seems to get any older. He looks about the same now as he did when he came to the big leagues. He still seems to approach the game with the same enthusiasm. He likes to play baseball. (In fairness, I should mention something else. He can hit. Anybody who can hit like Pete Rose *ought* to like to play baseball.)

Roy Campanella once said, "To be a big-league baseball player, you've got to be a man. But you've got to have a lot of little boy in you, too." I can't think of anybody who's better proof of that than Pete.

Pete is a pleasure to watch, not only because he's

talented but because he's not what baseball people call a "safety first" player. One reason that he looks so good, is that he's not afraid to look bad. If Pete Rose hits what some guys would call a long single, he's going to find out why it can't be a short double. He doesn't try to play a ball that's hit to him on the first hop until he's convinced that he can't catch it before it bounces. Pete Rose convinces hard, too.

If there is one thing that Pete can do as well as he can play baseball, it's talk. He's a big leaguer there, too. That's one good thing about this book. If you notice that Pete Rose skips from one subject to another when he writes, the explanation is very simple. He does the same thing when he talks. It's like Campy said, "He's got to have a lot of little boy in him, too."

But Pete Rose proves Roy Campanella was right about being a man, too. Pete Rose is a man. You'll see signs of that in this book, and I think you'll find them refreshing. One sign of being a man is to recognize that you're not an expert in every area that you might be interested in. He knows about baseball, and he doesn't hesitate to give you a clear picture of what he thinks is right and what he thinks is wrong. He doesn't have all the answers, though, for the things that bother him. Like the fact that the Montreal ball park is cold, for example.

Also, Pete Rose is not so impressed with himself that he misses being impressed with other people. That shows up in a lot of ways. Maybe it's how his mother-in-law fixes him chicken and dumplings. Or the feelings that Pete Rose has for his father, feelings that I'm sure you'll agree are justified after you read this book.

He really hits home for me when he talks about his one-time manager, Fred Hutchinson. "Hutch" was a tremendous man in the eyes of Pete Rose. He was a tremendous man in the eyes of Joe Garagiola, too. I knew Hutch long and well, and cherished his friendship. Pete describes his pain at Hutch's passing. I know that pain. I felt it, too.

I like this book because it doesn't just have Pete Rose's name on the cover—it's got Pete Rose inside, too. If you've never met him, you're in for quite an experience. If you know him as I do, you'll find yourself nodding and grinning as you read it.

Well, that's about all the warning you're entitled to. From now on, you're on your own, because here comes Charley Hustle.

The PETE ROSE Story

1 And then they said to me that it would be nice if I didn't use "ain't" so much in this book because kids may read this book and get the wrong idea of the English language. And they also said that they realized that baseball players, in the heat of the game, might be inclined to use cuss words but it would be better for this book if we left the cuss words out. So I said to them that was fine with me. And that is how this book got to the publisher in the first place. I do not pretend to be a brilliant writer. All I am is a baseball player and for my money, which is $100,000 a year, that is good enough for me.

So I took all the notes I had scribbled, paragraphs about this and that, and handed them to the editors in New York where they had a pretty girl go through and get rid of the "ain'ts." I guess I have been making notes on this book for two years. Sometimes I'd scribble a paragraph while I was riding on a plane to some game. Sometimes I'd scribble notes while I was watching television. Anyway, I ended up with more notes than I could shake a fist at, my wife put them in some kind of order, and when the publisher said, "Pete, have you ever thought about writing a book?" I showed them two cardboard boxes full of notes and said, "Listen, I think I have."

But on the other hand, I'm no Joe Namath when it comes to writing, I'll never be an Earl Lawson, and I don't think I'm a Jim Brosnan who is really James Patrick Brosnan and they called him the Professor because he pitched a lot and wrote a lot. He spent nine years as a pitcher in the majors, spending his time in Chicago and Cincinnati, and in those nine years he wrote books, won fifty-five games, and lost forty-seven games. But the real question is, what is *this* book going to be about? I guess it's going to be about me. But it's going to be about all those other people, too, the ones who helped me get where I am. I owe them more than I can ever repay. This book will be one way of thanking them.

A lot of people, back when I was named Rookie of the Year, figured I had reached a kind of peak. Some of them thought I wasn't going to be as good as I went around saying I was going to be. The way I say things makes me a little bit like Cassius Clay. Just like my newest prediction: about three years ago I told everybody that I was going to be the first $100,000-a-year ball player who didn't hit home runs or pitch thirty winning games. And now I am. Like, way back before then, I told people I was going to be Rookie of the Year. I told them in spring training that I was going to make the team in 1963. Don Blasingame (he is from Corinth, New York, and they called him the Blazer) had just finished the best year of his career at second in Cincinnati, so when I said that would be my slot, they all laughed. Only everything happened as I said. Maybe I said that stuff in a cocky way but I didn't mean it cocky. I believe in myself. I believe in myself real hard. If *that* is being cocky, I figure that is being cocky the right way. I think I *know* baseball pretty well. I think I know *me* pretty well. But I'll be fair about this. I may know me and baseball pretty well, but there sure is a lot of other stuff in the world where I don't know from nothing—and I don't go around pretending to know it. Okay? In other words, when it comes to something besides baseball, the only thing I know is to keep my mouth shut and my ears open.

What I'd really like to do, other than please you with this book, is hit .300 for ten straight years. I'd like to have a bunch of 200-hit years under my belt before they send me out to pasture. I think Ty Cobb had nine or something like that. If you hit .300 for ten straight years you get a chance at the Baseball Hall of Fame. I'd sure like that. Any player would. Any player out there today who doesn't want to end in the Baseball Hall of Fame should turn in his uniform and quit. I really mean that. The only thing I don't understand is how they vote the players in sometimes. I'd like to be the kind of player that makes the Hall of Fame the first time around. Some guys get in the running three or four times before they make it. Then, there's this business of putting guys that are retired in there. They deserve it, sure, but look at it this way. He should have got in while he was hot. I'm thinking of my friend Waite Hoyt. He made it when he was seventy years old. Waite should have been in the Hall of Fame long ago. Well, I'm just pleased that he made it. Waite is one the the finest gentlemen baseball ever saw. But this book isn't going to be filled with too many gripes about some of the things in baseball. Baseball has been too good for me for me to be that way with it. I'll leave most of the sour grapes for the ones who get their kicks that way. I'd like this to be a *nice* book.

Will I end up with some fantastic batting average like Ty Cobb had? His lifetime average was .367; in

1911 it was .420; and in 1912 it was .410. Man, I'll never be able to equal him because the baseball he played is not the game we play today. Back then, they didn't have the pitching we got now. Even Ty Cobb, if he was batting today, wouldn't hit .350. I'm at .309 now and I've got .312, .313, .348, and .335. It's tougher these days. I bat about 600 times a year. One year I went to bat 670 times. That's a lot of times at bat and you have to get a lot of hits to keep in there. Ty Cobb, of course, went to bat not as much a year as I did. In 1919 he went to bat 497 times. In 1923 he went to bat 556 times; in 1924, 625 times; after twenty-four years in the game he had been to bat 11,437 times, not counting 65 other times in three different World Series. But, as I say, the game has changed. Since 1930 the batting averages have gone steadily down, from an overall average of .290 for all the major league players to an overall average in 1968 of .230. On the other hand, we're getting more home runs, but I'm not. From 1876 to 1930, at best you'd see one home run per game. During World War Two home-run hitting declined even more, but then it picked up and now the average is nearly two home runs per game. The game has improved. There used to be at least a dozen errors per game when the game first started in 1876. That's when the records started, that is. In the 1930s, there were three errors per average game. Now we're down to about 1.5 errors per game. But pitching is what tells the tale. In the period between 1920 and 1940 there were about three strikeouts for each nine innings; now there are twice that many. And look at the use of relief pitchers. Between 1876 and 1915, they hardly used any. Then they started using about two relief pitchers a game (that's one for each team, I guess) up to around 1945. Now you'll see at least three relief pitchers used. All it takes is a hot relief pitcher to cool off a hot Ty Cobb until the Ty Cobbs aren't any more. So that's why I'll never match what that great guy did, no matter how much I'd like to or no matter how hard I'll try. It just isn't in the game these days the way it used to be.

Aw, don't look at me like that. Don't think I'm going to go around in this book shoveling a bunch of statistics at you. There'll be more than enough statistics in this book to please (I hope) the guys who love numbers, but on the other hand, this book is going to be about other stuff like how my dad got me started in the game, what umpires talk about, and how it feels to be down there playing in the bush leagues, eating your heart out, wishing for the majors. Like, right here, I want to thank the guys in the newspapers and in the broadcast booths because they're the ones who helped me make it in the majors. I like reporters. Some ballplayers don't. Newsmen bent over backward to be lenient in their judgment of me, but they don't hesitate to nail me when I do wrong, and I don't blame them when they do. There's Pat Harmon and Lou Smith and Bill Ford and Earl Lawson—and listen, I should name the whole roster but this would end up a telephone book, wouldn't it? Too many players want the cream. They won't take the bad with the good. Me, I hope for the good but when the bad comes along and the reporters write it that way, it's not their fault, it's mine. I've seen one player punch a sports writer but I'd never do that. Because you make an error and the guy says you lost the game is no reason to punch him. Listen, those guys in the press box could write tomorrow that I'm a bum and I'd still love them. They've been good to me. How can I forget that? The minute I do I hope somebody reminds me and gives my ego a boot in the tail.

Also, this book will be about traveling. And spring training. Listen, the first couple of weeks at spring training I go to bed pooped. We usually work out from 10 till noon, then eat, then back at 1:30 to around 3:30. Then maybe I'll take some extra practice myself and by six I'm back at the Tampa motel, exhausted. I'll stay in and watch the boob tube for the news. I dig television. At home we've got them all over the house. I'm one of these nuts who can't go to sleep until the movie is actually over. If there's a movie on, I've got to stay up until "The End" flashes on the tube. That's when we're playing night games during the season, of course. I can sleep late. Isn't that grand? Friday and Saturday nights in Cincinnati are the nights I hate and it's all Bob Shreve's fault because I think he's the greatest. He's host of those all-night movies and he always saves the best movie till last. We even set the alarm once for 4 A.M. so we could get up and watch his movie. So if we don't do well this season, don't blame the Reds. Take it out on Bob Shreve.

Or blame the Cool Ghoul on WXIX, the UHF channel. I really dig him. And I get a big kick out of Jim Nabors as Gomer Pyle. I like Red Skeleton, too. "Laugh-In" I always watch and I watch "Hee-Haw," too. I'd rather watch some of this stuff on the tube than go out for a big evening on the town. That figures, though. Usually I'm too tired to go out. Or I'm resting up for a big one coming up. Give me a chance to play baseball or see a movie that has monsters in it and I'm sitting on top of the world.

Being on television myself is okay, but I'm not the greatest and I'll be the first to admit that. The Reds are always sending us players out for television appearances to celebrate Bat Day or Ball Day or Jockstrap Day or something. I don't mind. Anything that promotes the game I'll do. Like there was the time I was on Bob Braun's show at noon over WLW. They had some girls there presenting Bob with Hawaiian leis and giving him a big smooch when they did it, so when I came on I presented him with a lei, too, and gave him a kiss, and he went nuts. He's really okay, isn't he? Bob is one of the finest guys we've got on the tube around here. He's a good-looking guy and I've got him wearing Hyde Park Clothes which is fine because when I'm not playing baseball I'm vice-president of that. I've met Ruth Lyons and been on the show when she was there. I was scared to death to appear because she's a real smart cookie but she loves baseball and went out of her way to make me feel at home. That woman has real class, hasn't she?

Now and then I appear on television commercials or in magazine ads. Harry Berns with Beatrice Foods up there in Chicago used me in a milk commercial. I also did a Milk Duds commercial for them. My wife made a mustard commercial. We've both made them for Rubel Rye Bread. And for Jack Meyers I made a few for Partridge Wieners. Now that Johnny Bench and I have that Lincoln-Mercury dealership in Kettering, Ohio, I'll probably be doing commercials for myself. But beer commercials? Cigarette commercials? Thanks but no thanks. I don't smoke. And as for beer, it's fine, but I would rather not do a commercial for anything I wouldn't want kids to go out and buy. It isn't that I'm a prude, it's just that I'm me, and that's the way I feel. I like sporting goods, though. I should. I'm on the MacGregor Advisory Staff, because I used their gloves and they help me and I help them. They're a good bunch out there, Bob Rickey and all of them. But I'm more baseball-minded than I am commercial-minded. And I can never do a Brylcreem commercial because I got this crew cut and I got this cowlick and it would take more than a little dab to do me.

Are you beginning to get an idea what this book will be about? I ramble, but that's the way I am. And there are a lot of people I want you to meet, like my dad, because if you can't like him, you can't like anybody. I've done a lot of growing up in baseball and maybe this book will show you some of it. In fact, there will be everything in this book but the kitchen sink.

There will be a chapter on me as a kid down there in Sedamsville and Anderson Ferry in Cincinnati. I want you to meet my kid brother who played house ball with me till we were both blue in the face. He's in Vietnam now and I hope he comes back safe and sound. If ever you drive out U.S. 50 west out of Cincinnati, slow down as you go by Anderson Ferry because that neighborhood—with its Schulte's Gardens and its Trolley Tavern and its ferryboats—is kind of sacred to me. That's where I grew up. And take it easy as you go by Bold Face Park in Sedamsville because that's where I first started switch-hitting. It was in the Knot Hole League, which is like Little League. Anyway, in Bold Face Park is where it all began, so honk as you go by. My dad used to play there when *he* was a kid. That shows you how long we've been around that neighborhood.

You're going to meet my dad all through this book because if it wasn't for him loving sports he might never have passed that love along to me. I'll never be the guy he is, but I keep trying to follow in his footsteps. You'll like my dad, as I said. As I say in the book, he wasn't one of these goody-goody types. He never taught me that jazz about it being how you play the game and not if you win or lose. Winning was his baby. He passed that along to me. So any hustle I have I got from him. I don't deserve the credit. He does.

In here, too, you'll find a world that was more innocent than the world we have now. This was the world when my dad himself was a kid. He did things—like sail the Ohio River in a leaky homemade johnboat— that he would never let me do. And I did things, like hitchhike, which I'm not about to let my own kids do. But that more innocent world was a part of my growing up the same as Knot Hole baseball was. I'll pass along to the kids some of the baseball tricks my dad passed along to me. Who knows? You might end up another Pete Rose—or is the world ready yet for another Pete Rose?

Western Hills High School is where I went—and spent five years getting through its four grades. This is a moment I'm not exactly proud of because I goofed off when it came to hitting the books, but it is all part of me, so I'll put in about that, too. I played football at Western Hills, was the runt of the litter, but I had a ball. Western Hills High School, which is a public school, never beat its archrival Elder High School, which was a neighboring Roman Catholic School for guys. Well, Western Hills never beat them much but this will be about the times they did, so that should make the Western Hills Alumni Association happy at least. Nobody was too happy with me there academically. I was the tough little nut from Anderson Ferry. If a guy shoved me accidentally in the school corridor, I belted him. So you can see why I didn't win too many scholastic honors, even though I was there one year longer than the average guy and I had an extra year to try.

High school, for a while, was a dim period of my

growing up and I almost took the wrong path and ended up nowhere. But this will be about how the teachers at school helped me and how my dad was during my low days. They all deserve the credit for shaping me up and getting me back on the right track. Maybe there's some kid at Western Hills—or some other high school—right now doing all the dumb things I did. If there is, I hope he reads this. I'm no preacher, but I've been there, so maybe reading this will help him a little. A lot of people helped me, so I'd be a nothing if I didn't pass along that help, wouldn't I?

Also, in this book, I'm going to go into this business of why—in Cincinnati—I think the Catholic high schools have and always will have better football teams than the public schools. Some of you may not agree, some of you may get angry, but I've got to tell how I personally feel about this because, as I say, I've been there and know whereof I speak. On the other hand, when it comes to algebra, you can tell me anything.

The first time I ever wore the uniform of the Cincinnati Reds? That's in the book and it's not when you think it is.

Will you sit in with me and my dad when I'm fresh out of high school and I sign my *first* baseball contract? Then I want you to fly with me—in the tourist section—to Geneva, New York, where for the first time in my life I meet up with a real professional baseball team. Sure, it's a farm club—out there in the bushes—but it was big time for me. I wasn't ready for Geneva, Geneva wasn't ready for me, the reports they sent back on me were terrible, but come to Geneva with me anyway and see what a rookie ballplayer goes through. It's not all peaches and cream, I'll assure you, but on the other hand it was the first time I was ever away from home, which—come to think of it—made it more exciting and more sad.

You'll meet Phil Seghi of the Cincinnati Reds. He's afraid to fly—flying scares the pants off him—but he's not afraid to take chances on rookies like me who think they know baseball but end up realizing they've got everything to learn. He's a great guy. You'll meet him all through the book. Up at Geneva, we'll both run into Tony Perez for the first time. And we'll run into the problem I posed: I was the brash local hotshot fresh from high school and he was a seasoned second baseman and there wasn't room on that bag for the two of us.

Actually you'll meet so many guys from Latin America in this book, you'll see why one of the guys in the Geneva boardinghouse complained, "On a clear night up here you can hear the Cubans yelling at one another."

My poor, poor dad. The first time he visited me in the farm system almost broke his heart. He learned I wasn't doing anything right. They told him, sadly, that the only thing I had going for me was the way I hustled. Yeah, my dad went through a lot to see his dream come true: his son playing in the majors. There were a lot of times that it looked like I wasn't going to get there. I'll tell about those times because they make up a big part of the story. Compared to Perez in Geneva I was all thumbs. I wasn't a good defensive player. I was only adequate at second base. Yeah, I went through some trying times up there in Geneva. But I did have, as I say, hustle. And I guess the way I slid headfirst into the bases made them look kindly on me. They must have figured that any guy trying to kill himself for baseball couldn't be all bad.

Then there's Tampa. Maybe you'll like coming to spring training with me or running around, growing up, in the farm system. That, to me, was really the big time: showing up in Tampa. I didn't do much sight-seeing. I stayed at the ball park and worked my tail off. The Gulf of Mexico was around somewhere, but I didn't look at it much. I'd visit Ybor City, the Cuban section of Tampa, now and then with my dad, but most of the time found me working. After the regular practice, I'd practice some more. Well, the farm system has changed a little since I was in it and it's changing even more—and I've got some thoughts on the system which I'll tell you about. I may be right or I may be wrong, but at least I'll speak my piece. All I'm suggesting is, the farm system isn't what it used to be and it never will be again. I'll go into that more later on. Stick around.

The farm system is where I first ran into Dave Bristol and his wad of tobacco. And that's where I first ran into Fred Hutchinson. Great guys, both of them, only now Fred Hutchinson is dead and the day he died I was out of the country, riding a bus, and they announced it on the radio, and the guy sitting next to me cried. I'll try to say good-bye to Fred Hutchinson in this book but I know right now I won't be able to do a good job of it. I'm not good with words and he deserves only the best words there are.

There are many lonely moments in baseball—in the majors as well as in the bush leagues. One of them is seeing a guy that has been released and sent back to nowhere, standing around, watching the other guys go on practicing, and all he has in his future is a bus to catch. There are a lot of funny moments, too. I'll go into some of the tricks that ballplayers play on one another. I'll go into some of the crazy things we do. I'll even be brave and talk about umpires because I like the guys, and I'll tell some of the conversations we have at the plate or while we're standing around out there in the field, waiting for the pitch. Did you know there is an umpire who *sings* to me? There is—and I'll even tell you the song.

My first year in the majors? Well, you can come along and go through that first year with me even though it wasn't the greatest year I ever had. Still, I got named Rookie of the Year, only I was in the army when they named me that and I couldn't celebrate; I had to go on mopping the floor because, as we all know, that is the way the army is. Be there at the plate with me the first time I come to bat in my first game in the majors. Nothing sensational will happen —I get walked—but it's a moment I'll never forget. No ballplayer ever forgets his first time at bat in the majors, though a lot of them wish they could. My first time at bat found the umpire sorry I was there. So come along to the first game with me.

My first major league hit was off Bob Friend. That's in the book, too.

Some of the National League parks we'll visit won't be there any more, like the old park in Houston where the mosquitoes sometimes outnumbered the fans. Freeze with me in San Francisco. Freeze with me in Montreal. Listen, I'm a warm-weather player and I don't dig this cold jazz. Come with me to Venezuela where the ushers carry submachine guns to keep the fans under control and come with me to Chicago where, in the Wrigley Field bleachers, nobody keeps nobody under control. I'll tell you all about those wonderful Chicago bleacher bums and why—even though they throw everything at me that isn't nailed down— I still think they're the greatest. After all, with them in the bleachers when I'm playing in Chicago, it saves me a trip to the zoo.

Why do I slide most of the time headfirst? I'll explain that as best I can and who knows? Maybe some Knot Holer or Little Leaguer will want to start doing it, too. I don't pretend to be the greatest baseball authority there is, but what I have learned (the hard way) I'll try to pass along to you, whether you're small fry on the team, manager of a small-fry team, or just a fan who thinks I do everything the wrong way.

I suppose I'll talk about slumps, too. Since there's no way to avoid them in the game I suppose there's no way to avoid them in a book about the game.

Also, come along to the army with me. Did I get special treatment or was I treated as one of the guys? I'll tell you what happened and let you make up your own mind. I'll even tell you about the time I marched my platoon into a ditch. And I'll tell you how to make iced tea for a hundred guys. You didn't realize I was so well versed, did you? Neither does my mother, so don't feel too bad. If you're about to go into the army I have only one piece of advice. Say "Sir" a lot. They get a big kick out of that kind of thing.

My second year in the majors was, I suppose, about the worst year I had. I had a rough time my sophomore year at Western Hills High School—and flunked—and my sophomore year in the majors wasn't a winner, either. I pulled a lot of time on the bench. I was really in the dumps. That's when I went south for the winter, to Venezuela, to play baseball and sharpen up. I sure needed sharpening. There was actually a moment that second year when I thought I was going to be shipped back down to the minors. It never happened but back then I had no way of knowing. That was, also, the last year of Fred Hutchinson.

He died before I ever got to play a good year and show him that his faith in me had been justified. So join me my second year here in the book. It will not be the greatest year but it happened so it's a part of the story, too. It would be dumb if I wrote nothing but the stuff in here that makes me look good. I can't make myself look perfect because that's one thing I'm not. If you don't believe me, ask my wife.

Race relationships—black and white or Spanish and Yankee—don't bother me but there *is* a problem in the majors and sometimes things aren't as nice as we'd like to believe. So I'll go into some of the things that happened to me. Happily, it all worked out for the best but as I say, no one is perfect. And neither is the game of baseball or the guys who play in it.

Also, I have a few suggestions for the general managers of baseball teams on how to get along better with the players. I figure if I can pass along bum advice to the small fry, I can pass along bum advice to the front office, too. The front office, on the other hand, keeps giving me advice, like, "Pete, we wish you would quit throwing baseballs into the stands." Only I keep on throwing—not hard, just gentle tosses— baseballs back into the stands for the fans and the front office keeps saying they're going to take the price of the balls from my check. So you see, we all give advice to each other and who knows? Maybe someday one of us will listen, but in the meanwhile, there's no hard feelings.

We'll go through each season together and you'll meet a lot of nice guys—many with real class—like Big Dee Spencer, Bill Mazeroski, Frank Robinson, Curly Smart, Vada Pinson, Ted Kluszewski, Sparky Anderson, Reggie Otero, and a bunch of others, including Joe DiMaggio who—if you promise not to tell

—once gave me a shower and I once gave him a shower but that was in Vietnam where we were on a tour, saying hello to the guys fighting over there. I grew up a lot during that Vietnam visit and that will be in the book, too, because that was a powerful moment in my life. They let me shoot off a few guns but I didn't hurt anybody and they let me run one of the gunboats down there on the Mekong Delta and I was careful not to run it aground. But, kidding aside, Joe DiMaggio and I met many brave guys in the military hospitals and some of their stories were enough to break your heart. You've got to meet these guys because, to me, they are the greatest.

You'll meet Gaylord Perry, too, who is a very nice fellow except when you're at bat and he's on the mound and then I don't care for him too much.

Well, I guess by now you're getting an idea of what kind of book this is. It will be the smattering of everything from the bunch of notes I have accumulated. Some of the stuff will be very personal. It will be the kind of stuff my wife—who looks like a million dollars in a minidress—will say I shouldn't say, like her looking like a million dollars in a minidress. But I figure if I'm going to put out a book about me and you are going to put out the effort to read it, I shouldn't hold anything back. I hustle on the field and I hustle here. In this book, this is the way things are. Or, at least this is the way things are to me. I'm not about to be a great pundit and tell the world how to run itself. All I know is baseball and as for the rest, I'm no expert and I don't pretend to be.

If you thought you were going to be mentioned in the book and I didn't mention you, I'm sorry. If I mentioned everybody who was ever kind to me this book would be as big as the Manhattan telephone directory. I've slighted no one intentionally. Okay? So now that I've given you fair warning, here we go. This book contains everything about me but the kitchen sink with the exception of the "ain'ts" which that pretty girl in New York has edited out, unless of course she wasn't looking hard and missed a few. But she's too smart for that. She ain't about to let that happen.

2 "I realize," my dad told the Knot Hole manager, "that you might run into a championship game, facing a right-handed pitcher. But I want Pete to bat left-handed against every right-hander, no matter what. I want your word you'll let him switch. . . ."

That was in 1950 when I was nine years old and trying out for my first team.

But I had checked in, of course, to the human lineup nine years before that—in 1942—the year after Boston changed its name from the Bees back to the Braves, the Japanese bombed Pearl Harbor, the hit song was "Hut-Sut Rawlson," the Reds under Bill McKechnie had finished third, and Detroit's Hank Greenberg belted out two home runs to beat the New York Yankees 7 to 4, only to be drafted into the army the next day. I was born the year after Joe DiMaggio had ended a fifty-six game batting streak when he went hitless against the Cleveland Indians. They say when Joe ended his streak, he sighed and said, "I'm tickled to death it's over."

And there I was, beginning.

By the time I was aware of World War Two, the war was practically a memory. So the childhood I went through was okay.

I mean that. Listen, I grew up attending every game the Cincinnati Reds played. When my dad didn't lug me out to the ball park I would be sitting at home, glued to the radio, tuned in on the action. School days were a different matter but there you are. And when I wasn't attending the baseball games, in person or by radio, I was *playing* in them—in my imagination, of course.

My little brother and I played house ball, bouncing a rubber ball off the red-brick wall at Schulte's, the fish place at Anderson Ferry. Morning, noon, and as far into the night as our mother would allow, that's where you'd have found my brother and me. We played so much house ball against that old red-brick building that I think we wore the paint away and that every six months or so, they'd have to repaint the building. I could be wrong, though, on that. You know how childhood memories are.

My poor brother, five years younger than I was, would pitch. But the bigger I got, the closer he would stand, so his pitches would be hard to hit.

When we weren't playing house ball, we collected empty pop bottles and turned them in for cold cash. Or, we stole watermelons. Or, I rode the ferryboat, *Boone Number Seven,* that rickety side-wheeler connection between Ohio and Kentucky. Or, me and some guys my age were up on the steep Ohio hillside, looking down into our river valley community, sometimes camping there all night. In the morning we'd eat bacon we'd cooked by campfire and we'd watch the river mist evaporate to let the Kentucky hills—across the river—come back from whatever place the fog had hidden them. Or, we'd play along the riverbank itself at the ferry landing. But most of the time, there I'd be, in Schulte's parking lot, dodging custom-

ers who came to eat his wonderful fish dinners, and
I'd be pretending I was with the Cincinnati Reds.

Anderson Ferry, the community where I was
raised, is an old-fashioned kind of crossroads settle-
ment a handful of miles west in the river valley from
downtown Cincinnati. The community is locked in
the narrow valley. Indians used to cross the river here
long before the first ferry began. Some say that during the Civil War this is the point Morgan's Raiders
entered Ohio to rampage through the countryside.
I'm not sure. History was never my meat. All I can tell
you is the valley on the Ohio side of the river where
I grew up was, at that point, only two streets wide.
Then it ends with a thud, blocked by a steep hill. Railroad trains—the Baltimore and Ohio as well as the
Penn Central (we used to call it the Big Four)—whistle west through this cramped valley on their way
west. The valley is grimy and noisy and fun.

Our particular community, called Anderson Ferry
because the ferry is there, never was a terribly rich
place. The area is known mostly for the ferry, Schulte's where I bounced the rubber ball and where people
came from all over to eat the lake trout, and—now—
a fancy kind of restaurant called the Trolley Tavern
and the Flying Bridge, both being a crazy mixture of
streetcar and riverboat stuff. When the guys and me
would camp overnight in the hills that hemmed our
valley in, we'd go first to Schulte's. Henry Lapp—he's
dead now—and Ken Rudusell, both of whom worked
at the fish restaurant, would give us French fries to
go camping with. Hey, those were the good old days.
There used to be a bus driver who'd pick us up on
nights we were supposed to be camping (but didn't
really feel like it) and we'd ride his owl bus to the end
of the line at Saylor Park and back again up into the

city. We would spent the night with him, just riding.

The old neighborhood is full of memories for me. I remember when the Trolley Tavern caught fire. I remember George Wells, an ex-fireman who worked for an elevator company, up there on the roof of the restaurant, chopping holes in it. I remember when the Texaco river terminal caught fire. The fire hoses, strung across the railroad track, were okay till a freight train whistled through. Then every hose was cut. I remember that fire real well because I was playing baseball when the first gasoline tank exploded. And I remember the awful night a guy got killed by a train at Anderson Ferry. He had been walking up the track, drunk as seven hundred dollars, when along came the train and it knocked him right out of his shoes.

But I guess most of all I remember baseball because baseball was all that mattered to me. I remember playing backyard baseball with my two sisters—Jackie and Caryle—and my cousin Lois. Listen, my sister Jackie was a pretty sharp little ballplayer. I remember that wherever I went as a kid—camping, exploring the riverbank, or sneaking rides on the owl bus—I always had a baseball glove hooked to my belt.

By the time I was nine, as I said, I graduated from the red-brick wall at Schulte's to what any kid would consider the big time. I was on a baseball team for real. The team was the Sedamsville Civic Club, I was the catcher, and the place we played was Bold Face Park in Sedamsville, within hollering distance of the Penn Central freight yards and the Ohio River where towboats were.

Being a Knot Hole catcher was the greatest thing that ever happened to me. At least, back then. But I still say that no games will ever be as wonderful as those house-ball games me and my brother played in Schulte's parking lot. I wonder what makes the remembering of childhood, though, seem so sad? I mean, it's like thinking back and remembering a baseball team that has been scattered nine different ways and isn't any more.

What kind of folks did I have? Well, in this day and age when kids are supposed to reject their folks, or put them down every chance they get, I suppose I'm a square. I happen to think my folks are the greatest. My mother can get along with anybody. She's that wonderful. If you can't get along with her, face it, you just can't get along. She is a wonderful mother. Now she's an even more wonderful grandmother. When God made her, He broke the mold.

My dad? I've got to tell you about him because he's about the most important guy in my life. This will be hard to do but let me try to tell about him this way. Right across from the Trolley Tavern was the Trolley Tavern football field. In the winter my dad played football there. In the summer my dad played baseball there. He played for a bunch of teams like Trolley Tavern, Tresler Oil, the Mohawks, the *old* Bengals, and Saylor Park. He was a heck of an athlete. A lot of people will argue with you all day that my dad was the best football player Cincinnati ever had. My dad played football till he was forty-two years old. My mother used to kid him and say that if he didn't quit football, she was going to leave him. She loves that guy. But who wouldn't love a forty-two-year-old football player who went out every Sunday and knocked heads with guys half his age? My biggest thrill back in those days was being the water boy on my dad's team.

That's when my mother worked at the Trolley Tavern, only back then they called the place the Twin Trolleys. I can still remember sitting in that place on chilly Sunday afternoons after my dad had played football. My dad and the guys would be sitting there, proud and dirty, in their uniforms, when they had uniforms, and right there with them at my dad's elbow was me, the team's water boy, drinking a Coke while the team tried to get outside a half barrel of beer.

I seriously believe from reading the newspaper stories about my dad and from hearing guys who played football with him that if my dad was a young man today and could have gone to college, he'd end up an All-American. I mean that. Anyway, sitting there in the tavern on those noisy and beery Sunday afternoons, surrounded by my dad and the other guys, I learned a lot. I can still hear him hammering at me:

"If you don't win, Pete, you haven't accomplished anything."

So you might say that any hustle I got in me, I inherited from that King of Hustle, my dad.

What kind of guy is my dad today? He's a rock. As I get this down on paper, he's fifty-eight years old. But to look at him, you'd swear he was only forty-four. He's not fat at all. He's got steel gray hair. He stands five feet eleven. He weights 190 pounds. He's a sharper dresser than I am. And even though he's a grandfather, he still hustles. He never walks when he can run. Only the other day I saw him crossing the Fountain Square plaza downtown. He looked at his watch and I guess he was late for an appointment because all of a sudden he took off at a trot. I get the biggest kick out of him. He passed guys much younger than him, left them eating dust. I'm glad for one thing, that those junior executive types with their sunlamp suntans didn't try to keep up with him. They wouldn't have stood a chance. All I know is, the day he stops hustling will be the day he dies.

He's not a drinking man, either. I've never once seen my dad drink hard liquor. I've never once seen him smoke a cigarette. He smokes cigars, though, after a fashion. Mostly he never lights them. He chews them to death. You might say I don't come from a drinking family. Come to my house right now, or to my dad's, and the most you'll find is some beer. When a football game is on the tube my dad likes his beer. My mother doesn't drink at all, but she smokes. And on holidays she'll mix a bunch of frozen Daiquiris—and that's about the size of it. Who drinks the Daiquiris? Friends who drop in. What I suppose I mean is, our family doesn't need booze to get high. We got each other, there's a lot of exuberance going, and who needs booze?

I'll be honest here. There was one time back then, when I was a kid, that I got drunk. One afternoon after one of his football games, my dad and me were over in Kentucky in this neighborhood tavern where the losing team popped for a half barrel of beer. I was going to be a big man so I sneaked beer from my dad when he wasn't looking. Trouble is, before we got home, I got as sick as I'd ever been. I threw up in two states.

After that I was more than willing to stick with the milk my mother gave us at our meals. Or, when I was daring and wanted to act grown-up, I used to drink a lot of tea. But beer? Not on your life!

Nonetheless, my dad let *me* do things that I would never let my kids, when they reach that age, do. Like hitchhiking. Our folks, if they knew about it, didn't seem to mind. Or, like we'd be gone for hours at a time, strolling along the bank of the Ohio River, exploring and playing among the driftwood tangles, chasing the river rats away. On the other hand, his folks let him do things he never let me do. I guess each generation of kids gets less and less freedom. Like, my dad when he was a kid growing up in Sedamsville used to get with other guys and they'd swim naked in the Ohio River, clear out to the middle of it. Like, he used to steal tomatoes from a farmer who lived across the river in Kentucky but who farmed a patch of land on the Ohio side down by Southside Avenue.

"Sometimes when I was young," he told me once, "we used to row old johnboats out to midstream where the stern-wheelers were. We'd wait till a stern-wheeler passed—the *Hubbard* or the *Ottawa* or the *Chippewa*—and we'd try to scoot in behind it to ride the first 'roller' the big wooden wheel made. Some of those 'rollers' when you got down in them were so big you couldn't see the hills on either side of the river."

But would my dad let *me* do that?

"No, Pete," he said. "Ride the ferry all you want. But don't you go fooling around out there in the middle of the river in some old johnboat."

Times sure do change, though.

Now, when *my* kids reach the age I was back then, I won't even let them play along the riverbank by themselves. Who knows what kind of guy they might run into down there? And I won't let them mingle with transients, either. All in all, I had an easier childhood than my kids will have, but my dad had an easier one than me. Like this business of transients.

"When they were building the Riverside roundhouse in Sedamsville," my dad said, "they brought in a bunch of Mexican laborers. These guys lived in rickety work trains in old day coaches they didn't use any more on passenger runs. These guys had a kind of ranch there, with donkeys, all fenced in. Most of them couldn't speak English. But every Sunday they'd go up to Bold Face Park and have crap games in the swimming pool the park emptied over every weekend. I'd start out, just standing around, watching. Pretty soon, one of the guys would see me standing there, he'd slip me a quarter, I'd get in the game, too, and stay in it till the stakes got too high. They'd end up shooting for four or five dollars instead of dimes and quarters. They actually had three different crap games going at once in the pool and everybody was shouting Mexican things at everybody else. One guy always stood up outside the pool, though, keeping an eye out for the law."

Yeah, my dad had a real good childhood.

Only one Saturday afternoon when a couple of guys and me were chewing the fat about hopping a freight train and taking a ride somewhere, my dad overheard us, and he put his foot down hard.

"None of that," he said.

"Why?" I complained. "You said you used to do it when you were a kid."

And he had done it, too. When he was growing up on Southside Avenue, right there by the Penn Central yards, he used to hop freight trains all the time. Only not from right there. He hopped them down the road at a place called Hampton Place where the freight trains sat, waiting to get out of the yards and go on to the main line.

"My mother never worried about me doing that," he told me later. "And I always felt I could handle myself. But even so, I did things I never want you to do, like hop those freights. We used to have a football team that practiced in Hampton Place near the tracks. But sometimes instead of practicing we'd hop a freight that went west into Indiana. We'd ride as far as Greensburg, beyond Guilford Hill, get off, and hop another freight back. We'd always be home by noon or one o'clock. We used to do that a couple times a week. Our mothers said nothing. . . ."

That was the way my dad was, but this is the way my dad was, too. Once when I was little he went downtown to a shoe store with just enough money to buy my sister a pair of shoes. But he never bought those shoes. He saw a pair of miniature boxing gloves —kid size—in a store window. He bought them for me. But when he got home from town and said what he had done, you should have seen the look on my mother's face.

"I'm glad about one thing," my dad said, recalling the look on my mother's face. "I'm glad they were miniature gloves. If those boxing gloves had been regulation size I think your mother would have put them on herself and given me a real going-over."

My mother wasn't that way—actually, I never heard them fight at all—but on the other hand for an hour or so after he came back from his shopping spree she was kind of put out at him.

I keep saying my dad is the finest athlete I'll ever know. He keeps saying he isn't.

"I really was never much of a baseball player," he said one time in an interview. "Oh sure, I loved the game when I was younger, but Pete is the *natural-born* baseball player in this family. His ability doesn't come from me. It comes from his mother's side of the family. My brother-in-law—Ed (Buddy) Bloebaum—is just about the greatest there ever was. When he got his first chance to turn pro he was playing with guys lots older than he was in the K. I. O.

League. He even played on the New Arrow team that won the league championship in 1920. He happens to be one of those guys who can do anything on the field and look good while he's doing it. When they first offered him a shot at the big time, he wouldn't consider it. Right then he was managing a pool hall at Fifth and Elm here in Cincinnati. Later on, though, he did go out and play a year at Cedar Rapids."

Between my dad and my uncle, who is now with the National Cash Register Company in Dayton, Ohio, I had baseball running out of my ears—and loved it. So if I happened to look good when I was a kid, I can't honestly take any credit for that. Listen, I had two of the best baseball teachers God ever put on the earth: that uncle of mine and my dad. But back then I sometimes wondered which they loved more, baseball or me.

There'll be more about this uncle of mine later because he played a big part in my baseball career. I want to give him the full credit he deserves. He went out of his way to make me look better than I really was. Even so, I'll never be able to thank him enough. I'm a little better, I guess, at baseball than I'll ever be with words. It is a time like this—when I honestly want to show my appreciation—that I'm sorry I didn't pay more attention to the English lessons they tried to lay on me at Western Hills High School. But I did my time at Western Hills, looking out the window on mellow spring days, dreaming of sports.

That makes sense, though. The dream of my dad was sports, too. Why is it some dads have to pass along their dreams, unrealized, to their kids? What I mean is, except for playing his heart out whenever he played, the only thing my dad has to show for *his* dream is a dumb kid like me who hustles on walks the way some batters hustle on singles. The trouble is, my dad never had the time for sports that I had. He went to old Woodward High School, in downtown Cincinnati, and they hadn't finished building Western Hills High School when he started. Well, they opened Western Hills High School in 1928. When they did, they asked my dad and the other kids from Sedamsville if they wanted to transfer and be the first class to graduate from Western Hills. My dad said no. So he stuck it out at old Woodward.

Every night after school and every Saturday, too, he worked as a delivery boy for a paper company. He hit the books a lot harder than I ever did. His teachers had convinced him—and rightly so, he still says—that if he failed high school he would be a bum for the rest of his life. So between working and hitting the books, my dad never even got to *see* a high-school football game all the time he was going to school. Sad, isn't it?

That's one reason I've got to keep hustling, don't you see? I've got to give my dad, through me, all the moments he never had time for when he, himself, was a kid. If I didn't hustle out there every minute, I'd be letting him down something awful. I let him down once when I was in Western Hills High School and almost broke his heart, but that's in the next chapter.

All I know is, he sure kept me busy when I was a kid at baseball. When I wasn't at Bold Face Park, playing with the Knot Hole team, I was in our backyard or Schulte's parking lot, having batting practice with my dad. He was—and still is—sure some teacher.

He'd work and work at me, making me bat left-handed. There he'd stand twenty feet away and say, "Never take your eyes off the ball, Pete." He kept harping on that at me. "Keep your eye on the ball,

Pete. Any time you're doing anything in baseball, keep your eye on the ball." Before pitching one at me he'd stand there, for as long as three or four minutes, moving the ball this way and that. And, during that time, if he ever caught me not watching the ball, he'd say, "Okay, Pete, you're not looking."

Keep your eye on the ball. Listen, I carry that habit with me today in every game. I watch that ball straight into the catcher's glove. On the other hand, I've seen a lot of players at bat take their eyes off the ball. They'll watch the pitch coming at them and if somewhere halfway it looks like it's going to be a bad pitch, they'll let up. Well, maybe it's going to be a bad pitch or maybe—at the last fraction of a second—it's going to turn out to be a good one. The only sure way to know is to keep your eye on the ball. I learned that from my dad.

I learned other things, too, like when the two of us would be tossing a basketball around. My dad would say, "Listen, Pete, whenever you're out in the court practicing with a basketball, throw the ball with your left hand. Don't worry about your right hand. Your right hand will develop naturally." So I used to practice that way with my left hand every chance I got. I still do. I don't pretend to be the greatest lefty in the world, but I hope I'm pretty good at it. I can do a lot of things with my left hand that most right-handed athletes can't. Why? Not because I'm the greatest, but because my dad is. That's the way he taught me.

Well, anyway, I graduated from the red brick wall at Schulte's to a catching position on the Sedamsville Civic Club's Knot Hole team. Although I went to Saylor Park Elementary School, I never played there much. Most of the guys on the team went to the Riverside-Harrison School at Sedamsville. Where I lived at

Anderson Ferry was the dividing line for which school you went to. As far as I was concerned, the real baseball action was not in Saylor Park but in Bold Face Park in Sedamsville. They always seemed to have better teams. I'm not sure why. Sedamsville, Riverside, and Anderson Ferry—where I lived— weren't exactly the richest neighborhoods Cincinnati had. In fact, they were pretty far down on the economic list. These neighborhoods were considered poor when my dad was a kid and time never improved them much. Saylor Park, on the other hand, was a place of nice homes that had big green lawns and fathers who shipped their kids, ready or not, off to college. Saylor Park was filled with second- and third-generation middle-class people, nice and well scrubbed and reasonably well heeled financially. Sedamsville and Riverside and Anderson Ferry were filled with second- and third-generation poor.

So there I was, on my first baseball team, playing in Bold Face Park where, years before, my dad had shot craps with Mexican laborers. Another guy there at the same time I was, was Eddie Brinkman who is now playing shortstop for the Washington Senators. And there I was, catching. Why? Because that's the spot my dad said where the action was. Listen, he's right. I think every kid going into baseball today should have the privilege—and it *is* a privilege—of spending at least one season behind the plate. Being a catcher matures you mentally and physically—fast.

Actually, I think I started as a catcher not only because of my dad but because of my uncle, the one I've got to tell you about pretty soon. He influenced me as much as my dad did. So there I was, a nine-year-old catcher, and there stood my dad and my uncle, getting their heads together, and saying to themselves, "It's high time this kid learns to be a switch-hitter."

The handwriting was on the wall. They were going to make me a professional baseball player or they were going to get me killed in the process.

"Pete," my Dad said, "we want you to catch."

"Me?" I said.

Back then the idea of catching didn't exactly make me want to turn handsprings.

"There are less good catchers in professional baseball than anything else," my uncle said.

"But *me?*" I said.

"You," they both said—and there I was, catching.

It was either be a catcher or look dumb in their eyes, and I loved them too much for that.

And I can still remember, standing off to one side, wishing I was somewhere else, as my dad said to the coach:

"I realize that you might run into a championship game, facing a right-handed pitcher. But I want Pete to bat left-handed against every right-hander, no matter what. I want your word you'll let him switch. He'll probably be weak left-handed. But I want your word that if you want Pete to play for you, he's got to be a switcher."

After a long silence during which a freight train whistled in the Riverside yards and started off, with wild huffing and puffing, to Indianapolis, the coach said:

"Okay, fine. You got yourself a deal."

The pattern, that long-ago afternoon, was formed. Now I can never remember *ever* batting right-handed off a right-handed pitcher. You might say that I've been switch-hitting since I was nine. My dad was right. "The advantage of being a switch-hitter," he told me that afternoon in Bold Face Park, "is that the curve will be coming at you instead of away from you."

I started as a catcher. When I played for the Delhi Eagles under Glenn Carter in the Delhi ball club the next year I was still working behind the plate. But also, now and then, I'd play third base, too. They figured that I was too small—"puny," one of them complained—to work the plate. I *was* small, too. Super small—that's how one guy said it. Listen, when I graduated from high school I weighed only 150 pounds.

What do I remember about my very first year in baseball at Bold Face Park? Not much, really. Yet, a lot of things. I do remember that when I started my first game, my dad gave up participating in sports for keeps. No more Sunday football with guys half his age. No more playing softball with the guys. "You're the athlete," he said. "Now I can watch you. . . ." I do remember, also, that at the end of the season we got jackets because we were consolation champions or something. Those jackets were beauties. I know because I wanted to sleep in mine. I wore it everywhere. That's how much I loved it. And I do remember, every game he could attend, there would stand my dad, watching every move I made, and I made some pretty dumb ones. I could read his lips clear across the field and they always said the same thing, over and over and over, "Hustle, Pete. Keep up the hustle. . . ."

And there's one special moment I remember. It concerns my grandfather. He lived in Sedamsville, always played solitaire, and was forever telling me about the time he hit a baseball so hard that it sailed clear out of Bold Face Park, cleared the railroad yards, and landed on the river where it hit a stern-wheel steamboat, causing the boat to sink. Only he was dying from cancer all the time I knew him. The day our Knot Hole team played the championship game at Bold Face Park, he insisted that my dad help him out of bed, down the stairs, and across the street to the park so he could see me play. I can still see him, standing on the sidelines, my dad supporting him, and he was shielding his eyes against the sun, watching. I'm glad we won that game. I'm glad we won for the sake of the team and for another—more personal— reason. I loved that old man, shielding his eyes, watching me play. I didn't know that would be the last time he would ever be out of bed. I didn't know that after the game he would go home to die.

When he died, a part of childhood—for me—seemed over.

And Bold Face Park—to me—was never the same again.

3 They might call me a "showboater" now when I play for the Reds, but I can't claim to win all the prizes for hustle. All anybody has to do is look at my record—scholastic, that is—in Western Hills High School. Talk about something deflating a guy's ego! Most guys go through high school in four years. It took me five. I was so involved in sports in high school that I let the studies slide. I'm not proud of that. I point it out just to show you that I'm not as great as some people say I am. In high school I forgot to hustle academically. I slowed down. Well, I've learned my lesson. I've been running ever since.

I started in high school in 1955. They sprung me in 1960. I started the summer after Birdie Tebbetts found his Reds ending the season in fifth place. By the time I graduated the Reds had run through several managers: Birdie Tebbetts, Jimmie Dykes, and Mayo Smith. The year I got out of high school Fred Hutchinson was running the show. The team itself hovered out of the money in those years. In 1955, as I said, the Reds finished fifth; in 1956, the Reds finished third; in 1957, fourth; 1958, fourth; 1959, tied for fifth; and in 1960—after I was out of school and signed by the Reds —the team finished sixth.

When I started at Western Hills High School in the

ninth grade, I was the sports addict from Anderson
Ferry. I went out for everything but the girls' swimming team. In my freshman year, I played football,
basketball, and baseball. I was having a ball. Glenn
Carter, the guy I played for in Delhi, had his son on
the varsity. His son was our freshman coach. In baseball I was a catcher. I was a guard in basketball. And
in football they put me in the half back position. I had
a good year in football but the coach worried a lot. I
was so little—and such a lightweight—he was afraid
to use me because he thought I might get creamed. No
matter. I made first string and for a couple of games
I was captain of the team. Charlie Schott, the nephew
of Jake Schott who is chief of police, was on the team,
too. He turned out to be a heck of a player.

My poor dad, though. He'll never forget the first
time he watched that freshman football team.

"He didn't get in the game," my dad later told a
reporter when asked about my performance in that
first scrimmage. "And there I stood, thinking to myself, 'What goes on here? My Pete can play better than
a lot of those guys. Why isn't he in there?' The next
game the same thing happened. Actually I began to
get a little mad. I wondered if I should go up to the
coach. But something told me to keep my mouth shut.
Later on that week, after the second freshman game,
I was talking to a fellow whose son played on the
team and who was a little closer to the situation. I
asked him about why they weren't letting Pete play.
He said he had wondered the same thing. He had even
asked the coach. The coach had told him, 'I'm just
afraid to put that kid in there. He's so damned little,
he might get hurt.'"

"How did you react to that?" the reporter asked my
dad.

"I was sure mixed up," my dad said. "Here the coach was more worried about Pete's safety than I was. I had been wanting to throw my boy to the wolves. . . ."

I *did* get to play, as I said, and that was all—to me —that mattered. Editor's note: also, that I didn't get killed.

Yeah, that first year at Western Hills High School was beautiful. It seemed like everything was going my way. I figured I had the world by the tail. Only when I went back for my sophomore year, everything fell apart. They didn't ask me to play varsity football. They didn't come out with a letter of intent. Listen, by the time school started in September, 1956, I wasn't the happiest guy Anderson Ferry had ever produced. I was really fed up.

Result: I did a lot of dumb things that I regret even today. Maybe I shouldn't put stuff like that in a book like this. But I've got to be honest with your or nothing makes sense. Now and then a guy will come out and write something about my being a know-it-all and so on. I'm not. And the sophomore year at Western Hills High School proves it. I had a lot to learn then. I've still got a lot to learn. That's why, I guess, I keep hustling. I'm still trying to make up for goofing off.

What I'm trying to say is I'd start out for school and I'd never get there.

That shows how dumb I was.

Or, I'd go to school a half a day and then, with a couple of other guys, cut out. Where'd we go? Bum around. Go downtown, see a movie, or just bum. The guys felt they'd got the same bum deal. Yeah, we really went around in those days feeling sorry for each other. When we got together we weren't helping anybody. I think that's the only thing I really regret in my whole life, that I wasn't a good scholar the way my dad was. But I think I could have been if I had wanted to be. Only I was too interested in feeling sorry for myself.

If I wasn't bumming around out of school, I was messing around in school. For a while that year I spent more time in the assistant principal's office than I did in class. It wasn't that I did anything terribly wild or awful. I'd get caught for being late for classes because I'd dawdle in the corridors between periods. Or, maybe I'd nail somebody with a rubber band in one of the classes—and the teacher would send me to the office. Or, there were fights. Nothing great or dramatic. No rumbles. Just plain ordinary fights. Listen, I used to get into a lot of fights. I don't know why, though. Maybe it's because I came from a rougher neighborhood than most of the other kids came from. What I was doing, really, was taking out on everybody else the hard time I had caused. Things went from bad to worse.

On afternoons I could look across Ferguson Road to the athletic field and see the team practice—whether it was football or baseball made no difference—only there I sat in the principal's office, trapped and left out of everything. Those were, I think, the loneliest afternoons I ever spent. I was never more out of it.

So I'd skip school more.

I was going the wrong way fast—and that's for sure.

Each day that year seemed lonelier than the one before. I thought I was fooling my mother and my dad. I thought I was fooling everybody. The only guy I ended up fooling was myself.

Every morning, so things would look good, I would be out bright-eyed and bushy-tailed, waiting for the school bus. The school-bus route started right by the Trolley Tavern so I had my choice of any seat on the bus because I was the first passenger. I used to save a front seat by the window for this one girl. We'd talk as the bus filled up. But the more the bus was filled with kids, loaded down with books, and the more noise they made, the more silent I became. By the time the bus—crammed with kids—swung into the loop in front of Western Hills High School, I would be as silent as a tomb. Everybody, it seemed, was making it at school but me. I'd follow the gang inside the building and maybe I'd go to class or maybe I wouldn't.

My dad got called to school lots of times. That broke my heart. Each time I would promise to straighten up. Only I'd look out the window of the algebra class, see the squads go through scrimmage, and I'd get fed up all over again.

My mother? She was sad but she said nothing. She left matters like that to my dad.

And my dad had read me the riot act so much, what he said lost meaning.

Things came to a head at the end of that sophomore year. I flunked. Simple as that. I had goofed up completely. About the only thing I got a good grade in was gym. But what good is an A in gym when the rest of the grades would be nothings? Listen, that year I even flunked study hall—or, if they had given a grade in it, I would have flunked it. Yeah, I was a real winner.

That summer I played baseball—of course. And that fall, when I went back to school to have another go at my sophomore year, I hustled the books as hard as I ever hustled on any ball diamond. The result: I grew up a lot, I got on some of the teams, and I was on the right track again. It scares me, though, to think of the kids I see now—the dropouts—hanging around street corners these days, forever on the edge of things. Any one of them could have been me. I was that close to flushing everything down the drain. Anyway, my *second* sophomore year I played football and baseball. They never did let me play basketball for the varsity. They took one look at me and decided I was too small for that action.

Two years of varsity football. Yeah, those were the days!

The year I played is the last time Western Hills High School beat Elder High School. For those of you who are not familiar that much with Cincinnati, Western Hills and Elder High Schools, being neighbors in the western suburbs of my hometown, were archenemies. Elder was the all-boys Catholic high school. That section of town would get real excited about Thanksgiving Day. Turkey was almost in second place in popularity to the Western Hills–Elder game each Thanksgiving morning. Western Hills High School never won many of the games. That's why I'm kind of proud to say the last time Western Hills beat Elder I was on the Western Hills team. We beat them worse than any team in the history of the battle ever beat them. The final score was 34 to 14. It was a cold, icy day. I'll never forget that. I scored nine points in that game: one touchdown and I kicked an extra point and ran an extra one. That was the year Western Hills High School shared the Public High School League Championship with Hughes. We won seven, lost two, and tied one.

That was sure some team. I played right halfback. Charlie Schott, nephew of the police chief, was left halfback. Ralph Grieser, who later went on to Michigan, was quarterback. Walt Dietz was at center. And we had a little guy, littler than me, Rudy Lengardo, a defensive man. Jake Schott, Jr., son of the police chief, was the punter and he ran the punts back with me.

But the game I remember most with those guys was the game we played against Hamilton Public. They beat us 24 to 22. Maury Bibent, whose dad owns the Tiny Cove Restaurant in Cheviot, was on the team, then, too. I think I ran three touchdowns that day. On one punt I remember I was one man away from going all the way for my fourth touchdown and old butterfingers me, I fumbled the ball, and they went on to beat us as I said. That was sure a depressing moment for me. I was the place kicker, I kicked off, I also ran the punts back, and I kicked the extra point. I was sure having a good night when, with fifteen seconds left in the game, I was all set to kick a 42-yard field goal. Only it never happened. The coach let Maury Bibent kick it. He missed, probably the same as I would have missed, and that was that. We'd lost the game. It wasn't Maury's fault. Listen, for a kid in high school to kick a 42-yard field goal, he'd have to be pretty good. And that's a fact.

I remember another football game where we beat Withrow High School. We beat them 60 to 6, but I got nothing to brag about there because I didn't score a single touchdown that game. And I played the whole game, too. I did score three or four extra points, though. But Jake Schott sure had a field day. He was scoring touchdowns for Western Hills every time we turned around. His dad wasn't the chief of police then. He was just a colonel on the force. His dad and my dad used to sit together on the wooden bleachers and yell like a couple of kids. They were really something.

Only that game I didn't give *my* dad much to yell about. I'd be running up and down the field, having a great time, but whenever we got near the goal line, they'd get somebody else to take over. So what? The team won. That, to me, was the important thing. It is the same way with me today. I'd rather have our team win than me end up a hero—and our team lose.

That was a beautiful year for football at Western Hills High School. We beat Central 26 to 0. We beat Woodward, my dad's old alma mater, 36 to 0. We beat Taft 14 to 6. But Hughes turned around and beat us 40 to 22. They blocked two punts that game and, within a minute of each punt, they ran them out and scored touchdowns against us on both of them.

The craziest game I played when I was at Western Hills High School was the time we played football against Central. I actually ran 120 yards for a touchdown. Listen, I was running all over the field. You can actually count ten guys touching me on the highlights film they replayed of that run. It was only a 50-yard distance between me and the goal, but it was a screen pass. I started out on one side, went back to the other, went back again—and then scooted down the sidelines like greased lightning. So you see, I actually went back and forth twice. One guy—Charlie Nickerson—made two and a half blocks on that play. He threw one block, got up and went back and knocked another guy out, and as I was streaking along for the touchdown, he was well into his third block.

After I came off the field, the coach said, "Hey, Pete, what did they grease you with before that play?"

I was too pooped to say anything. Running 120 yards for a touchdown can take a lot out of a guy.

But I'll never forget that run if I live to be a million years old.

But the games between Western Hills High School and Elder are the ones a guy remembers, especially if he's from the western section of Cincinnati. So when I was on the team that beat Elder in 1958, I was real proud. A couple of years ago my brother, playing for Western Hills High School, ran back a kickoff 90 yards for a touchdown. Up to that time he did that and the last time I had played, only two touchdowns had been scored against Elder by Western Hills. You might say that when it comes to football, the guys from the Catholic high schools in Cincinnati are all aces.

I think this is so because in the Catholic schools they go all out for football. Listen, sometimes as many as 10,000 people would show up to see Elder High School play. At Western Hills High School we were lucky if our cheer leaders showed up. When Elder High School played Purcell High School, both being Catholic schools, they played at St. Xavier Stadium—and packed the place. It was standing room only. The same was true when they played Roger Bacon High School. That's what I call real enthusiasm.

Maybe it's because the football coaches in the Catholic high schools around here make good money. In the public high schools, the most the coaches make is about $500 above their regular salary. But the coaches in the Catholic high schools make as much, I'll bet you, as some of the coaches in some of the small colleges. I know one high-school coach that has offers from several colleges but he stays put. Why? More dough.

We used to have bull sessions in the locker room at Western Hills, trying to figure why the Catholic schools kept running over most of the public high school teams.

"Listen," one of the guys said, "it's a wonder we don't get killed out there. Some of those guys have been playing together since the seventh grade. And even before that. The grade schools are like minor leagues for Elder and that's a fact."

"Also," another guy put in, "Elder is strictly a boys' school. No chicks. It's tougher to get some of the guys here interested in sports. They're too busy making the scene with the gals. We got 1,500 nice-looking girls. That's what I call a distraction."

"One of them is fat, though," the first guy said. "She doesn't distract me."

"So that leaves 1,499 who do," we pointed out.

Yeah, we used to have all kinds of theories, like at Catholic high schools they didn't have secret fraternities. Western Hills High School wasn't supposed to have fraternities and sororities, but they were there. That can take up a lot of a guy's time. And every time you turned around, something else extracurricular was going on. Meanwhile, over at Elder, there sat the Catholic guys, nothing to hang them up, making sports their big deal.

But don't get the idea that because I went out for everything athletic I didn't have an eye out for the fair young ladies. As an outfielder—now no longer with the game—used to say, "Listen, you guys, there are two things I can do real well. One of them is not run into the wall when I'm chasing a fly ball and the other is inventory every pretty young thing in the stands that day." As you know, I *have* run into walls out there. So I'm not as good as that guy, but you see what I mean. What I mean is, it wasn't all locker-room jazz at high school.

After the games at high school there would be these canteens where the guys and the gals would hang out. And always, within spitting distance of Western Hills High School, there was that drive-in called Frisch's where they sold double-decked hamburgers. After each game the restaurant always held more people that it could hold—and that's a fact. Everybody was filling up on Cokes and Big Boys, as the sandwiches are called, and a few would be crying in their malteds because Western Hills had blown another game. It was a real noisy and wonderful high school hangout. The places smelled of French fries, hamburgers, girls' perfume, and milk shakes. That was living. The place is still there. And it is still *the* place for the Western Hills High School bunch.

Since most of the time I didn't have too much money, I wouldn't exactly go inside, but I would drive through the parking lot a lot. That used to burn up Reuben Frisch. Back then, he hated my guts and he had good reason. I would come in with fifteen cents and buy one coke—and spend the whole evening, taking up a booth. That used to gripe his soul. I've been kicked out of there more times than I can remember. Now he's retired and we're the best of friends. When I got started playing with the Cincinnati Reds, he couldn't figure that I was the same nut he used to chase out of his place.

"You sure have changed a lot," he told me once.

He was right, too. Back then, I was pretty much of a wise guy. I thought I had the world by the tail. And all the while I didn't know enough to come in out of the rain. I still don't. But you can't blame me for that. I remember playing in Cincinnati eight innings during a pouring-down rain. We were playing Pittsburgh, the season was near the end, and we just had to get the game in. That wasn't so bad, though. I remember one game we played in Candlestick Park where the fog was so thick I couldn't see from second base to Vada Pinson out there—somewhere—in center field.

It was a night game, the fog was rolling in over the mountains, but this has nothing to do with me back there in high school, does it?

About my *social* life. Well, as I said, I used to save a seat every day on the school bus for this one girl. Only I used to save a seat for this one guy, too. Pretty soon, they started going together and now they're married. They're the Ray Blacks. So you might say I wasn't exactly batting a thousand where the young ladies were concerned. There was another girl—well, sort of. What I mean is, I was about the only guy at Western Hills High School who had a *girl* bodyguard. She was a beautiful girl, too. I think she was a football queen or something. But she looked upon me as a brother, so what was the good of that? She wasn't really a bodyguard. She was my den mother. They appointed her to look after me and keep me out of trouble. I'd carry her books down the hall, meet her at her locker, and stuff like that. She worked in the office and Mr. Hobson used to tell her, "You watch him, Jean, and keep him straight." Her name was Jean Blankenship. We'd go to lunch together. We'd be most everywhere together. I guess they figured if I was carrying her books I wouldn't be able to go around decking people. It worked, too. She was a real beauty. She was beautiful inside and out. She was one of the top girls in the school. But she was older than me— and to her I was just a dumb kid brother. She was really okay. So much for any love life in Western Hills High School. It was there, but when it happened, I was always somewhere else, goofing off.

As for a *real* girl friend, I didn't have one until I was around sixteen or seventeen. I was too busy with baseball—and the other sports. Maybe if I was in high school now, things would be different. All I know is, that is the way things were and the way I was back then. Who knows what things will be like in another ten years? Maybe kids will start going steady in kindergarten. But I'm no authority on stuff like that. I can read a pitched ball pretty well. I can't read the future, though. The only place I'm smart—if I'm smart anywhere—is when I'm out there playing baseball. And even out there I'm surrounded by guys smarter than me. I have to hustle to keep up with everything. I mean that. All I'm really saying is, in high school I looked at an awful lot of pitchers, pitching everything at me but the kitchen sink. I'm not being corny and overly modest. Listen, I'm not *that* good. I have to be modest. I have an awful lot to be modest about. I'm no Joe DiMaggio, but let me say this. I once gave Joe a shower and he gave me one. Brood about that for a while. It happened in Vietnam. But that's much later. Meanwhile, there I was, back in high school, lucking out with grades.

But not with the girls.

By the time I reached my senior year at Western Hills High School I was pretty much back in everyone's good graces. My grades weren't the kind that had universities outbidding each other to get me signed up as a scholar, but they were pretty good. My dad stopped worrying about me turning into a bum. My mother stopped worrying, too. The three of us figured I would at least be a high-school graduate.

"There were times, though . . ." my dad used to say, thinking back then.

Yeah, I know exactly what he meant. There were times when both of them—and me, too—figured I was never going to get any kind of diploma. That's why my senior year was pretty nice. I was at least making it. Listen, that was a good feeling. Not to be making it,

I can tell you from personal experience, is the loneliest feeling they got in this world.

The only sad part of my senior year in high school was that I had shot my wad insofar as being eligible to play on any of the high-school teams. This was my fifth year in high school. This kept me off the football team and baseball team. I used to go out, help coach where I had anything to add, but that wasn't the same as playing. I don't dig sideline action. Only there I was, sidelined. It wasn't anyone's fault but my own. The sporting scene in Western Hills wasn't geared to guys who need five years instead of four to get through.

But I had a good thing going that senior year. I used to go down to the ball park where the Reds were playing, put on a Reds' uniform, and along with a handful of other high-school guys, we'd be out there in the field, catching fly balls during batting practice the Reds held. Hey, that was really something. I guess that was about the most important thing that happened to me my senior year. Other than getting that secondhand car that had no front bumper, that is. Does every guy fall in love with his first car? I know I did. I bought it for a hundred bucks off Larry Bloom. It was a 1937 Plymouth. It had a radio, a stick shift. It was dark blue. And it only had 35,000 miles on it. But it looked so funny without that front bumper that when I brought it home my mother looked out the window and laughed. Mothers don't know too much about cars, do they? Even though it had running boards she kept laughing because she just couldn't believe that I paid a hundred bucks for it. Anyway, there I was shagging fly balls at the Reds' batting practice. And there I was, wearing a Reds' uniform. That was the greatest, really.

"John Brosnan was responsible for Pete getting down to the ball park," my dad told an interviewer. "John knew more about kids who played ball at Western Hills High School than anybody else knew. John seemed to have his own personal encyclopedia on any kids who played ball at Western Hills or Elder or even in the Knot Hole Leagues. Listen, John knew each kid's family and each kid's history. He was always around for practice. If a kid hit a ball and it went out in the street at Western Hills, John would trot out and bring it back. See, he sort of worked for the Reds in a bird-dog kind of job. He was the one who fixed it so Pete could go down there afternoons and work out in a Reds' uniform. This was big stuff to me. The first afternoon Pete was down there, I rushed out to the ball park as soon as I got off from work. I didn't know then about getting in at the pass gate. I went to the front and asked the ticket seller how soon I could get into the park. He said they didn't open till six. And Pete had been there since four. So I paced up and down until six, went in, and there was Pete—in uniform. I choked up. You know, there was my boy in uniform. . . ."

The interviewer told me later that at this point in the interview my dad actually got tears in his eyes because of that memory. Can you see why I love my dad?

"I felt," my dad had told the interviewer, "that if Pete never takes another step in baseball, at least I saw him in a major-league uniform. . . ."

It was, my dad said, a beautiful moment.

The moments weren't always that beautiful, though. There was the time going to the park and putting on the uniform and pretending to be in the big time got to be old hat. I drove my car—with the running boards—over to see this girl instead of going to the park. But my dad showed up at the field, saw I wasn't there, so he telephoned my mother.

"What happened to Pete?" he said, hurt.

"I think," my mother said, "Pete said something about going over to a girl's house after school."

"Do you know their number?" my dad said. "Well, call him and tell him to get the hell to the ball park."

Forty-five minutes later, there I was in uniform, chasing flies.

And that was the day I first met Fred Hutchinson. I saw him from a distance. I was in the locker room when he walked through. The first meeting, if you'd call that a meeting, was most casual. No matter. He was to be, for me, just about the most important guy in the world. He was the guy who made the Big Time happen for me. And he was the guy who, when he died, broke the heart of everybody who loved baseball. He was a real man. He had class.

And that afternoon I almost missed, he nodded to me as he passed through the locker room.

I'll never forget that moment. And to think, I almost missed it completely because this chick had blue eyes and a funny way of cocking her head when she grinned.

4 "There is," said an outfielder I once knew, "contracts and, on the other hand, there is contracts."

True.

I suppose this year—1970—I was real proud to put my John Hancock on a contract that paid me *more* than $100,000 to do what I would have done anyway. But even so, I don't think any moment will equal the moment I signed my first contract with the Cincinnati Reds. That was in 1960. I had just graduated from Western Hills High School. I was still sleepy from the all-night way high-school graduates carry on. But the contract woke me up fast. If it hadn't have been for Uncle Buddy, though, none of this would ever have happened.

During my senior year in high school, since I was not eligible to play for the varsity because it was my fifth year at school, I played in the Dayton Amateur League. I was batting .500 in that Dayton League and I had already traded my 1937 Plymouth on a 1949 Chevrolet. I played in the Dayton League for a team from Lebanon, which was the only team in that league that wasn't located in Dayton itself. It was a Double A Amateur League. I was playing for Tommy Thompson, who is now a scout for the Washington

Senators. We played teams from Wright-Patterson Air Force Base and a bunch of others. A half dozen teams made up the league—and there we were, hustling, looking great, and in first place. During the day I'd be trying to knock algebra into my head. Then, after school, I'd take off for Dayton. Those were the days—and nights. Sonny Webb and George Thacker, two Negroes from Cincinnati, were my teammates. Sonny was a real good friend of Frank Robinson. That was as near as I got to *greatness* that year, but for me, that was near enough. *I* was playing with the friend of a great ballplayer whose flies I'd caught at the Reds' park during batting practice.

"That may not impress the girls at Western Hills," my dad told me once, "but that sure impresses the heck out of me."

What position did I play in Dayton? Mostly second base. We played three days a week: Mondays, Wednesdays, and Sundays. The first game I played everyone gave me funny looks. That figures. I looked like I was still wet behind the ears and playing out of my league. But there I was, playing second base. That first game I had to prove myself to just about everybody including the water boy. Well, on second base I got in on the business end of a couple of double plays. That made them start looking at me differently. I even got a base hit. After that game, I was sure psyched up. That's when Uncle Buddy—that wise old man—took me down a few pegs.

"Don't get all excited," he cautioned. "Listen, Pete, just relax and play."

That was hard advice to take, but I took it—and on the strength of that, I started tearing up that league. I was really grooving.

But my uncle had other irons for me in the fire. I

didn't know that at a lot of games there was a man named Jack Baker in the stands, giving me the once-over. He was a friend of my uncle. My uncle had taught him the tricks of the scouting game, so there he was, sitting in the stands, watching me play, and there he was, a scout for the Baltimore Orioles. Both he and my uncle, scouting for the Reds, watched me get five for five one day. That's when Baker said to my uncle:

"I'm having Newhauser, our head scout, come out and look at Pete the first chance he gets. Make sure the kid doesn't do anything till he hears from Baltimore."

Poor Jack Baker. He didn't know the Cincinnati Reds, via my uncle, were also kind of interested in me.

As for me, I knew none of this. I was out there, playing ball, and really having a time. And during the day, I could see all the pretty girls at Western Hills High School. Life was real good back then.

But then I graduated from high school and the world got even better. My dad knew what was happening behind the scenes, but I sure didn't.

"I knew the Orioles were interested in Pete," he told an interviewer once, "but I said nothing to Pete about it. His uncle, who knows more about these things than I did, and I figured that knowing about the Orioles might upset Pete's game. So the Friday night Pete was graduating from high school, the Reds had another one of their baseball clinics, this time up in Piqua. That's why I was surprised to see Pete's Uncle Buddy show up at our house, which is a long way from Piqua. . . ."

That must have been some meeting.

"I thought you were in Piqua," my dad told him.

"Well, I'm not," my Uncle Buddy said. "Got more important things to do."

"Like what?" my dad said.

"About Pete's future."

"But he's not here. He's out celebrating. You know how kids are on graduation night."

"Let's give him a little more to celebrate when he gets home," my uncle said. "The Reds want to talk to him about a contract."

"When?" my dad said, amazed.

"Like tomorrow morning," my uncle said.

And that was that.

That wonderful uncle of mine had given me the best graduation present anybody had ever given anybody anytime anywhere. But there was more behind-the-scenes dickering left to be dickered before we all got together in the office of the Reds the next day. I'll never forget that Saturday morning. I was pooped but I was also bright-eyed and bushy-tailed. Does that make good sense? It does to me.

First thing we did when my dad and I got to the park was take a look at the field. Suddenly I felt like maybe I was really a part of it, not just a kid from high school out there catching flies on schoolday afternoons with a bunch of other guys. That old park never looked better than it did that morning. I remember that my dad and I walked out along the field, somebody—I forgot who—was in uniform, working out. I remember my dad picking up a ball in right field and tossing it back in. I wonder what *his* thoughts were that day? Neither one of us said much. I was too awed to talk. But what do dads feel at times like that? Pride? Sure, but there must be more. My dad deserves all the good feelings God ever put on the face of this earth.

We saw my uncle in the stands talking to Phil Seghi,

who handles the business chores for the Reds. Finally
my uncle left Seghi and worked his way over to where
we dawdled.

"I think," my uncle said, "we're going to get $7,000
out of him."

"Is that good?" my Dad said.

"It's better than what the others are offering him as
of now," my uncle said. "They're offering Pete nothing."

"What about the Orioles?" my dad said.

"A bird in the hand is worth two Orioles in the
bush," my uncle said.

Some joke!

Ten minutes later I was sitting in on my first contract meeting. My uncle and my dad were there. So
was Phil Seghi. So was a guy named Boyle and a guy
named Smith. We sat around chewing the fat. Or
rather, they did. Mostly I listened. My uncle had been
right. They were willing to fork over $7,000 for me to
sign a contract. And, to sweeten the pot, they were
willing to pay another $5,000 if I went on a major-
league roster and managed to last thirty days. My
head was swimming with the thought of my new
riches. But my dad was saying:

"I'm not sure about this. The reason I'm not sure is
I promised Jack Baker of the Orioles we wouldn't do
anything till he had a chance to talk with us."

There was a long silence.

"Well, Pete," my uncle finally said to my father, "if
that's all you're worried about, I'll talk with Jack. This
kind of thing happens all the time."

But *not* to me, I was thinking in near panic. I
thought the whole deal was going sailing out the window.

". . . The fact this kind of thing happens all the

time," my dad was saying, "doesn't make it right. I owe him the courtesy to talk with him."

Good-bye $7,000, I thought. Good-bye, Cincinnati Reds! A bird in the hand is worth ten zillion Orioles in the bush. That's what I wanted to say.

But I sat there, poker-faced, and said nothing.

Out of the blue, everyone was looking at me and my dad was saying gently, "Listen I shouldn't be making this decision at all. Pete, what do *you* think?"

Great guy!

"I'd like to sign," I said, surprised at how normal my voice sounded. "I'd like to sign and go right now. If, that is, this other thing . . ."

My dad helped me. "Buddy," he said to my uncle, "if you're sure Baker will accept this thing as all right, let's say yes. Okay?"

And that was that!

I think, though, I aged ten million years between the time we said we'd sign and the Reds said yes. The moment only lasted a microsecond, but for a kid like me, his future hanging there, it seemed like forever.

"Now, Pete," Mr. Seghi was saying, "you can do one of two things. You can go up to Geneva and play right away, or you can wait till next spring to sign, go down to Tampa, and start off even with everybody."

I started to answer but he went right on.

"I'll be honest with you, Pete. I know you've been playing ball a couple times a week, but you're going to have to face facts. You're really not in shape to play. Three times a week isn't enough. But if you want to go to Geneva, fine. We don't care if you go up there and hit only .100. What we really worry about is the effect it will have on you. After all, in Dayton you were tearing the league apart. It won't happen that way in Geneva because you're not ready. They'll be tearing *you* apart."

I digested this sad news.

"But, Pete," he said, "if that thought doesn't bother you and you still want to go, you can go."

Dumb me. Without hesitation I said, "I want to go right now."

The rest of them laughed.

"At least wait till Monday," Mr. Seghi grinned. "That's when the plane leaves."

I waited, but I'm an impatient guy. Between that Saturday and Monday seemed forever.

My dad and I went to the little golf course they got in Saylor Park and we played a little, but my mind wasn't on the game. And our telephone never stopped ringing. The news had been on the radio and there it was: hometown boy signs with Cincinati Reds. And there I was, Monday, waiting at the airport, for my very first plane trip anywhere. I was in seventh heaven when the plane zipped along the runway. Moments later Cincinnati was spread out before me, as far as the eye could see, but there were scattered clouds and there was haze. The last thing I saw before we vanished into the clouds and haze was that most beautiful of all sights: the Cincinnati Reds' baseball park. Then, once above the clouds, I turned my attention to the future (Geneva) and to the pleasures of the flight (the stewardess was a blonde and her eyes were green). Wow!

I thought about telling her I had just signed a contact to play with the Cincinnati Reds. Not exactly the Cincinnati Reds, but with the farm system, which to me back then was one and the same. I didn't get the chance to tell her, though. Some dumb baby started to cry and she had to go heat its bottle. If I had known the reports that were going to come back about me, I think I would have started crying, too. But I guess ballplayers don't cry. Especially when they're flying off to the future in a four-engined plane. I went to my future by way of Rochester. I went the rest of the way to Geneva by bus. Nobody rolled out any red carpet when I got there. I guess I was the only one who knew I was a hotshot.

And that first moment in Geneva I wasn't too sure of even that! The only thing I was sure of was, I wasn't going to live high off the hog. I was going to make $400 a month. And out of that I had to pay my living expenses, which means not many steak dinners. When we would be on the road they were going to pay our hotel bills—room only. They gave us three bucks a day to eat on. Listen, we almost qualified for the food stamp program, but we stayed. We weren't there to get fat. We were there because somewhere along the line we all fell in love with baseball—and that's the way love affairs are. You dream a lot, have highs and lows, and eat hamburgers.

In the major leagues they give you fifteen dollars a day for your food and laundry. But I'm talking about nine and ten years ago. That was when—let's see—we got $1.50 and $2 a day in Class B, $3 in Class A, $5 in Double A. That's why they say life in the bushes is tough. It's not all peaches and cream. Now in the majors, they give me twenty-five dollars a week for laundry and stuff. So I switched from steaks to hamburgers. But I sure saw a lot of hamburgers bite the dust before I had enough scratch on me to go around ordering steaks. This was back in the days they had six leagues in the bushes. Now they only got three.

But I'm getting ahead of my story, which shows you what kind of a book writer I am.

What I mean is, there I was, getting off the bus in Geneva, New York, away from home for the first time in my life, and like I said, there was no red carpet which is just as well because I wasn't expecting any.

Geneva, with less than 18,000 people, sits up there in the Lehigh Valley on the northern end of Lake Seneca. Rochester is about forty miles one way from it. Syracuse is about fifty miles the other way. Geneva is about thirty miles south of Lake Ontario. In other words, I was over five hundred miles away from the French fries at Schulte's at Anderson Ferry. That was the farthest I had ever been away from home. And I will be the first to admit I was probably the lonesomest and most homesick guy that year that Geneva ever had.

I went straight from the bus station to the ball park. I walked right up to that place, lugging my suitcase, and trying to forget how far away I was from those hometown French fries. Listen, I was about as far away from everything I had ever known as a guy could get. And everybody at that ball park seemed to be waiting for me, but they weren't waiting for me with open arms. To them I was that kid from the Reds' hometown. They had all got the word what a local "star" I had been. So you can see they weren't exactly pleased to see me.

They had good reason to feel that way, so I don't blame them. Tony Perez was up there having a great year at second base. But the first thing they did was move Tony over to third and let me have a chance at second. That's the kind of thing that doesn't win many friends. And to make matters worse, I wasn't exactly the polished baseball player that any of those guys were.

Look at baseball this way. There's a big fat difference between sandlot and professional ball. The guy on the sandlot goes out when the spirit moves him and if it looks like rain he sits home watching the boob tube. The professional is out there working up a sweat several hours every day, nearly every day of the week. He can't help but get better at the game, can he? The way I see it, playing in the Dayton League three games a week was better than playing in the American Legion League once or twice a week. It takes playing to make a good ballplayer better and that's a fact.

Well, anyway, there I stood like a country idiot at the ball park and there I was, getting distant looks from most of the guys. It wasn't the warmest welcome I had ever got, I'll clue you. The next thing that happened is a guy took me down to some hotel they had in Geneva and he checked me in. By that time twilight was coming, so he left me.

"See you at the park tomorrow," he said.

But he didn't sound too much like he meant it.

"Where are the other players staying?" I said.

He shrugged. "Around Geneva," he said. "Here, there, and everywhere. Most of them have been here a while, kid. They already got their living quarters. Besides, some of them ain't bonus players. They couldn't afford this."

Before I could tell him how things really were with me, he was gone, and so I went up to my room. Talk about mixed feelings. I wasn't about to quit but on the other hand, as I unpacked the suitcase my mother had packed for me, I sure wished she was around or dad was somewhere I could go and have a long walk with him. But everything was too far away. There I was in Geneva and all I had was baseball.

But baseball was enough. The next day I felt better and the moods changed. They had to. The first time I walked into the clubhouse, these five or six guys from Cuba were talking at each other a mile a minute, talking Cuban at each other, and that was sure something to hear. They didn't have stuff like that back at Anderson Ferry. They had to talk to each other that way because a couple of them didn't know a word of English. But they sure knew baseball.

Then I ran into Ron Flender. Now he's a guy I'd gone to Western Hills High School with. Only by the time we got together in Geneva he had got himself married. He was a right fielder. I hoped when I ran into him that we could room together but with him being married that was out of the question. So by the time the first full day was over, I found other accommodations. I moved in with three guys. One of them was a left-handed pitcher named Jack Irwin. There was another left-handed pitcher, too. He was John Truex, the guy who fell off a building in New York a couple years ago and got himself killed. Then there was one right-handed pitcher, Larry Souel. And me. We stayed at a house belonging to a guy named Mr. McGuire. We were within spitting distance of the ball park.

"On a clear night," one of the guys told me, "you can hear the Cubans yelling at each other."

After the first few days, I'd felt I'd been there all my life. Most of the guys were older than me but they took me in. A couple were first-year guys, the same as I was, but they had been there already and were really in good shape. Two and a half months of experience that year made the big fat difference between how good they looked and how dumb I looked. But the coaches up there treated me all right. Only they could tell I wasn't really progressing. My fielding was pretty good, but it wasn't sensational. My hitting, just like Mr. Seghi predicted, was way off. I was getting the blues fast.

Everybody on the team tried to cheer me up, but that didn't help me much. I mean, have you ever been cheered up by a bunch of Cubans who didn't know a word of English?

So I started taking extra practice every chance I got. I think that the key to good hitting is maturity. A guy just can't be a good hitter when he's young. He's got to mature. He can run around, look like a million dollars, but unless he's got some wisdom at the bat, he's really got nothing much at all. So the coaches tried to pound batting wisdom into me via extra practices. I was willing. Listen, I wasn't going anywhere. No dates. Nothing like that. They were paying me $400 a month and I was there, trying to look like I was earning it.

I didn't realize I wasn't improving as much as I thought I was. That was because I couldn't see the reports the farm club was sending back to the Cincinnati home office about me.

What happens is, every day the manager of each minor-league club files a report on what happened— the good stuff and the dumb stuff—that day. So along with the great things that were being reported about guys like Art Shamsky and Bobby Alaska, there would be sad things reported about me. But the important thing was, I was a professional ballplayer, traveling with a professional team. Every time I felt sad, I reminded myself of that. Later on, let me clue you to some of the crazy stuff that happens when a team travels, but right now I better keep on about how I almost blew everything by the way I was playing in Geneva.

Once my mother and dad drove clear up to Erie, Pennsylvania, to see me play. Luckily for me that year, we had about the best team in the league. I might not have looked good, but the team sure did. Well, I wasn't really doing too bad. I was hitting .277, which isn't bad for a second baseman but listen, against some of those pitchers I should have done a lot better. All I lacked, as I said, was wisdom at the plate. Anyway, there my folks were in the stands.

"How did Pete play that first game you saw him play in professional ball?" they asked my dad later.

"Gee," my Dad said. "I like to died. It amazed me how *good* those kids were. When I saw those kids play, even though they were young, I thought how good they are, but on the other hand, how far they are from the major leagues. I just couldn't believe what I was seeing. Then I saw how Pete was. He had improved, really improved. Like, he was hustling. And he was learning more than I could ever have taught him. Some of the other players didn't have Pete's hustle, though. I remember that during the course of the first game there was a ball hit out into left field. Up there they just have regular light poles up and the light poles stopped the ball. I was bothered, though, to see the fielder who was chasing the ball give up on it. The first chance I got after the game I asked Pete, 'Who was that guy who gave up out there?' Pete said it was Art Shamsky. Well, after I got to know Art better I found he was one of the nicest kids and he's the kind of guy who hustles but just looks like he's not hustling. So I never questioned his hustle again. Art does the best he can—and that's darned good. . . ."

My dad, in the interview, looked reflective. "Pete had been up there a month by the time I showed up. I had just gotten this Anglia, this English Ford, and was anxious to put some miles on it. I remember that we got to the ball park just as their bus was pulling in. It was around five at night. Pete was and wasn't expecting us. I had written him that I was coming up to see him but I wasn't sure when and no arrangements had been made to meet. Only when he climbed off the bus I could hear him shout, 'Hey, there's my dad and mother!' Only he had to go right in so we didn't get to talk with him actually until after the game."

Listen, if my dad knew—back then—how I wanted to talk to him right then. But that's the way baseball is. I know, though, that he would understand. His coming up there was a kind of turning point for me. It got me back on the track again.

My dad explained it in that interview.

"When the game was over that first night in Erie," my dad said, "I got the shock of my life because Pete was actually calling me down to the dugout. And there he was saying, 'Dad, I want you to meet our manager.' Then Pete said, 'I've got to take a shower. I'll be right out.' And he left me there with the manager. We must have been there only three minutes but in those three minutes I was told 5,000 things that were wrong with the way Pete was. This shocked me because I had thought that Pete was a pretty good ballplayer. But there the coach was, saying to me, 'Does he always do this this way, does he always do that? Does he always swing this way when he bats left-handed?' I was dumbfounded. I didn't know what to say. I think that finally I stuttered, 'Did you ever try him catching because Pete was a good catcher in high school?' And the conversation kind of dwindled away. Then Pete came back, fresh from the shower, and we talked about other things. If we had talked about what his manager had said, I think we could have broken his heart.

"Now that I think back there to that night in Erie, I think part of the reason the manager took this attitude was that Pete himself hadn't been ready for the Geneva club when he had signed. They had suggested he wait but he·hadn't even wanted to wait for a clean shirt. And I think the home office must have sent instructions up to Geneva, telling them that they're sending a local boy and they wanted him in the lineup right away. I can't blame the manager for thinking, 'I've got Tony Perez playing second up here and doing a fine job for me, but they send me a local hotdog and I got to put him in. So what do I tell Perez, the other kid?' Anyway, the manager was only there another month. The Reds sent him off on a scouting assignment and along came another one. This one and Pete got along real good. Pete wrote me that they were always hitting him ground balls in extra practice and . . . well, I guess the proof of the pudding is that the year up there ended pretty good for Pete. He ended up the most popular player on the team and he got the first gifts there he ever got in baseball: two Samsonite suitcases. He was sure proud of those. I was sure proud of him."

It's a wonder I lasted at all. I wasn't a good defensive player up there at the beginning. I was what you'd call only an adequate second baseman but I sure wasn't a spectacular one. Why? Because I never really had the practice at second base. Compared to Perez, I must have looked like I was all thumbs. But figure how long I had been playing before I went to Geneva.

Other than Knot Hole games and weekend stuff, I had played only two years in high school. Listen, when I joined the roster of the Reds for real, playing for Cincinnati, I had only about four and a half years of actual experience. And there I was playing second base for the Reds in a league where most second basemen have ten years of wisdom behind them. All I had behind me was hustle.

So there I was, having a ball, doing my headfirst slides into every base but home (listen, to slide headfirst into home plate is dangerous) and running to first each time they walked me. I did all the stuff I had been taught. I watched the ball every minute, right into the catcher's glove behind me. But all in all, I wasn't exactly the greatest. My size was against me, or so they thought. I had to hustle to prove I could keep up with the best of them. It was do or die for me in Geneva, and I wasn't about to die. Two months later Geneva was a memory. My first crack at professional baseball hadn't been an earthshaking event, but at least I was still around. That's more than a lot of them thought I was going to be.

I remember sitting around home, fresh from Geneva, and they had this football game going over there by the ferry. I ached to get out there and play.

"You might get hurt," my dad said, "and put an end to everything."

I said nothing.

"If you get hurt," my dad said, "the ball club is sure to find out about it. They might think they got themselves a pretty dumb athlete who goes out and hurts himself in a game of scrub football."

"Dad," I said.

"Yes?"

"What did *you* use to tell everybody?"

"When?" he said.

"When they said you were crazy, you the father of four kids, out there playing football with guys half your age. And they went around saying you'd be hurt. What did you used to tell them?"

He gave me a funny look. "I'd tell them that there isn't a man in the world who could hurt me on the football field. I'd tell them . . ."

He stopped and smiled.

"If I was like that," he said, "how can I expect you to be any different?"

"So?"

"Go on out there," he said, "and show them how it's played. Only, Pete, one thing."

"What's that?"

"Don't forget to hustle."

5 They go around saying that the minor leagues have changed, which could very well be true because everything else has and why should the bushes stay the way they were?

My dad was glad that I was still in professional baseball. He told me later, after I had been to Geneva, that the grimmest day he had in his life, outside of a death in the family, was the day in Cincinnati he had met someone from the Reds' front office. This guy had the scouting reports. My dad asked him how I was doing. The guy said nothing. He just handed my Dad one of the reports which said, "Pete Rose can't make a double play, can't throw, can't hit left-handed, and can't run."

My dad was shocked.

"Does it say that Pete does *anything* right?"

"Well," said the guy, "it does say that Pete seems to have a lot of aggressiveness. Does that help?"

"Not much," my dad said.

So you can see why he was as pleased as I was that after Geneva I was still on the roster. We were both pleased. He was not only pleased, he told me later, he was downright surprised.

After Geneva I got my contract. I was assigned to

the Jersey City baseball club, which had a working agreement at the time with the Reds. It used to be the Havana, Cuba, franchise, but by then Fidel Castro was making a mess of everything down there so the shooting match was moved to New Jersey, complete with the Cuban manager named Nat Reyes. The team I was with was 90 percent Negro, but that kind of stuff never bugged me. The other 10 percent were guys like me, still wet behind the ears, from Geneva.

So when my dad got to Tampa where we were working out, he found a pretty discouraged me. I was sure glad he showed up because right about then I felt I didn't have a friend in the world. He got right off the bus, tried to find a hotel, didn't, so he just wandered over to the ball park where I was.

"What's the problem, Pete?" he said.

I laid it out.

"The manager," I complained, "won't even let me pick up the bat. He keeps telling me to put the bat down and that he'll tell me when to bat."

My dad looked around the field in that hot Florida sun. The regularly scheduled afternoon rain had yet to arrive.

"And they all talk in Spanish," I complained. "Listen, I don't even know what they're talking about."

So my dad went over and settled in the empty stands. At least it was a comfort, knowing he was there. The afternoon wore on. Pretty soon, it was around three, quitting time, only I didn't quit with the rest of them. I walked over to my dad and said:

"Hey, how about hitting me some grounders?"

My dad, great as he is, is nonetheless an awful shy guy.

"Well, Pete," he said, "I'm not sure what your

manager will think of that. There *are* insurance regulations and if I went out there on the field with you and you got hurt . . ."

"Wait here," I told him. I went and asked the manager, who surprised me by saying yes, it was okay. And in English!

My dad later said that was one of his proudest moments, hitting me grounders on a Reds' field, even though it was in Tampa and not Cincinnati. He wore an old sports shirt and old pants and listen, my dad looked right at home, banging them out to me.

Tampa, Florida, was not another Geneva, New York. Instead of Lake Seneca, there was Tampa Bay and the Gulf of Mexico just beyond. I had never smelled salt air before. I had never been to Florida before. Listen, it's like I said. I had never been *anywhere* before I started professional baseball. My dad and I got the biggest kick out of wandering around Tampa. I was supposed to be in every night by midnight. After each practice, my dad and I would practice some more. Then we would go out and see the world. We used to go out and watch the dog races. We used to go to the jai alai games. We used to walk down to the docks where the banana boats docked. That was the first time I had seen an ocean freighter. Some of them were rusted hulks that didn't seem safe enough to go down the Ohio River, but they had come to Tampa from as far away as Japan. We got the biggest kick out of hearing the sailors—Japanese—jabber at one another. Down there, with my dad, was a whole new world. I saw more fishing boats than I knew they had. Everybody, it seemed, owned one. Or, if they didn't own a fishing boat, they owned a sailboat.

We used to visit Ybor City, which is the Cuban quarter in Tampa. That's a place of tenements, everybody speaking Spanish, lots of greasy little restaurants that sold black bean soup, and great huge warehouses with great iron windows where—inside each one—they were rolling cigars. I saw more things than I had time to write home about. At times it was the same as being in a foreign country. There were a lot of old people, too, around Tampa. Or, some would come over the causeway from Clearwater or St. Petersburg to sit in the sun and watch us play ball. Many of the old people were from Cincinnati. They had retired to Florida and seeing us was about the only *real* touch they would ever have again with home. They were beautiful old people, but in some way they always made me sad. It seemed like everybody had stopped loving them. That's the sad part about being down there in Florida. At times it is like being surrounded by thousands of ancient people who are sitting on park benches in the sun, waiting for their Social Security check or death. But the smell of the Gulf—salt water—was good. And so was the cry every afternoon of "Play baseball." After all, *I* hadn't come there to die. I had come there to begin. But still, the old people made me sad.

The minors, you see, were good. But they had their lonely moments. Now everybody says the minor leagues are changing. But the people in them aren't. The guys in the bushes are still hustling, grabbing for the brass ring. Like, in the Cincinnati farm system this year we got a kid named Wayne Simpson. He's a pitcher who is going to be a real shot in the arm for the club. He just got through pitching winter ball and he pitched seven shutouts. Our farm system is really producing for Cincinnati. Like, we got two shortstops who are real good defensive men: Frank Duffy and a guy from Venezuela named Dave Concepcion. I think

Wayne Simpson will be a starting pitcher for the Cincinnati ball club this year. Listen, he's got the personality and the temperament to be a good pitcher. He throws hard and he's a good athlete. There's probably a gang of young Pete Roses out there in the farm systems, itching to replace me, and I say more power to them. I'll just have to play that much harder.

Today, though, it seems like most of the farm systems use their money to get good pitchers to sign on the dotted line. That's because a pitcher matures faster than a hitter does. When I was in high school the clubs weren't exactly busting the door down to sign me. We both knew that. If it hadn't been for my uncle I'd still be on the outside, looking in. But consider the farm system of today. If the team has a farm system with, say, four teams in the minors, there will only be thirty or forty pitchers in the entire setup. But there will be carloads of outfielders. Each year more outfielders are traded than pitchers because you got outfielders crawling out of the woodwork. You watch the draft choice an see if I'm not right. Unless a team happens to *need* a third baseman and there's a hotshot available, they'll just try to trade a third baseman. They'll save their top draft choices for pitchers.

But they're right when they say the farm system is changing. I think the system is changing because of the expansion of television coverage of the big-league games. Why would people want to watch a minor-league team on the tube or in person when they can watch a good major league team on television? It's as simple as that. When I played in the farm system, we would draw over 100,000 a season. That's in the Triple A. Not any more, though. Everybody is at home, glued to the tube.

On the other hand, the farm system isn't going to

die of old age. The farm system is to baseball what colleges are to professional football. Professional football, in that respect, is lucky. They don't have to make any dollar investment in bringing the kids up. He gets his football schooling through his college. So you see, no matter how good you are in football, you'll have four years experience in those "minor" leagues before you get called to the majors, which is professional football. But baseball players are signed before any of this kind of apprenticeship. The ball clubs foot the bills for *our* schooling. And in the minors— whether in baseball bush leagues or in a campus schedule—some of the guys don't make it. I don't think, as of today, over a hundred players come out of the farm system in baseball each year. I guess each club doesn't pick up more than a dozen at the most. But I can remember when the scouts used to go bidding against one another. Only now they got this draft and the team that finished last gets first pick. I can remember when there were minor leagues all over the place, but not any more.

Maybe it's because kids either go into college or they get drafted into the army. Do you know that there are a lot of college guys who sign professional contracts and when they negociate the contracts, they make sure they get a college education first? So they go to college each year till June—and *then* they play baseball. But there are only a couple of schools that are really hotdog in the baseball department. The University of Cincinnati is one of them. So is Ohio State University. I think Ohio State ranks in there because they have that indoor field in Columbus. Then there's Southern California. There's U. C. L. A. They're the "good weather" schools. Also there's Arizona State. It always seems to have good baseball teams. But it happens like that because at some of these places they can play baseball all year round. On the other hand, up at Northwestern or the University of Indiana, well, it gets pretty cold sometimes in April and May. Anyway, it is as they keep saying, the minor leagues are changing. All I know about the bushes is when I was there.

In the minors they weren't down *too* much on my ability. Mostly they were down because of my size. But about every other week my uncle would go into the front office and convince them that our whole family was a family that went around maturing late. He told them not to worry too much because he figured sooner or later I would grow, too. My dad always told me a guy made his own chances and his own breaks. But growing bigger was one break I couldn't pull off. I had to substitute hustle for height.

I got off to a good start there in Tampa. By the time we had played fifteen games I had got a dozen triples —and the season was only a month old. So I was really getting the publicity. And there I was, batting .350. The publicity inspired me some but my mother inspired me most. When my mother was down there once in Florida she sat in the stands the day I tied my own record for triples. I took the ball from the third baseman and ran over to where she was and handed it to her. I ended that year with thirty triples, but the day my mother was there was the nicest of all thirty.

Since it was unbelievable for a guy to hit thirty triples they let me play in the instruction league the following year, hoping to groom me a little, because even with thirty triples under my belt, I still needed a lot of grooming. Played that winter, too, making the jump from Class D to Class A. I did better there than I ever did in high school. I skipped Class B and Class

C. The year I played in Tampa I was also named Minor League Player of the Year—in the Florida State League. Tommy Harper was the Minor League Player of the Year that same year in the Three I League at Topeka where he played under Dave Bristol. He was a second baseman same as I was, of course, and so was César Tovar, who had been named Minor League Player of the Year in the Pin League. So the Cincinnati Reds had not one but *three* second basemen who had been named players of the year. So the next year I played second base at Macon, Georgia, and Harper played second base at San Diego, which was Triple A. I got hot again, hitting seventeen triples that year, leading my league in triples as well as setting an all-time record for runs when I scored 136 runs in 138 games. Yeah, I was having a ball in the bushes—and not only that, I was learning a lot. I had just about reached the point where I knew how little I *did* know. I might have been a hotdog, but I got news for you, I was a hotdog who listened and tried to learned. I *had* to keep up the pace. There were too many good players around who were better than I was. If I relaxed one minute, I'd have been out of my ear. I was happy, though, in Macon with Dave Bristol. I hit .330 there. I got thirty-five doubles in addition to the seventeen triples. I think Bristol was kind of happy I was around, too.

Some of the guys like Harry Anderson thought I was doing good enough that year to be moved over to San Diego, but I guess they didn't want to push me along too fast. Whenever Dave Bristol heard that kind of talk, he would just look at me, chew his wad of tobacco, and spit.

I think he dug me because I liked the game as much as he did. He liked the way I didn't quit when the whistle blew. I'd stay around after the regular practice and work out with anybody who would work out with me. I had to. Listen, I was running real fast just to stand still in those days. And you want to know something? I haven't stopped running yet. Let the other guys go out and give 100 percent if they want. They're good. Me, I got to give *110 percent* to keep up with them. The minute I slack off, I've had it. Baseball is a hard game. Love it hard and it will love you back hard. Try to play it easy and ease off and the first thing you know, there you are, on the outside, looking in, wondering what went wrong.

Altogether, I played two and a half years in the minor leagues. That isn't long at all. Guys like Helms and Shamsky spent twice that long. Maybe I was lucky, skipping from a D to an A team because when you get up on an A team you are in a gang of guys that play pretty fast baseball. D was for the younger guys, which was me. C was for guys a shade better than the D. Then there was B, but A was the best. In those days not many guys jumped from D to A teams. Then I went from A into the majors, skipping Double A. That was hard to do back then, when there only ten teams. So, as I say, I spent two and a half years in the minors. First there was Geneva and after that I went to Tampa on this roster from the Jersey City team because everybody has got to be on a roster somewhere if he wants to get to spring training and he's not there on the major-league list. After that summer in Tampa I went to the instructional league because I still had a lot of learning to do, the next year I went to Macon, Georgia, and then I went to the instructional league again, and after that there I was suited up in the uniform of the Cincinnati Reds.

I had no great experience as an outfielder back

then. Since I worked a lot as a catcher for Dayton before I went to Geneva I wasn't exactly setting the world afire with the way I handled ground balls, either. When I went to Tampa I was just turning twenty years old—and there I was, playing with guys like Harry Anderson, who were ex-big-league players that had played Triple A and what they didn't know about baseball hadn't been invented yet.

They had the brains and ability and the *real* baseball wisdom. All I had was the idea of hustling and hoping. Yeah, now that I think back on it, I'm surprised I even lasted. Maybe they liked the way I was out there, running around like a chicken with its head cut off. Whatever the reason, I didn't get sent home— and that's good because that would have broken my heart. I really mean it.

But we sure used to have some great times. I had a good time with the guys and I had a good time when my dad got the chance to come around.

"I remember my first visit to Tampa to see Pete," my dad told an interviewer once. "I had been there around three days, hitting Pete a few after regular practice, only the team was due to play in Lakeland. I had no way to get there and I was feeling kind of blue about that, but I underestimated Pete. The first thing I know, he was standing there and saying, 'Would you like to come over to Lakeland? Our Jersey City team is going to play Denver.' Denver was a Detroit farm team. Pete said, 'I'm on the list to go over. Maybe I can get you a ride, too.' I said, 'Oh, no, Pete. Don't do that. I'd rather hang around here in Tampa by myself and watch the rest of them work out.' I didn't mean it but I didn't want to upset Pete. Only nothing would do but he got me a ride in the same station wagon he rode in. I felt uneasy, all of them being ballplayers, but they made me feel right at home.

"I was glad when I got over to Lakeland. It was the first time I had ever seen that complex layout with its four diamonds, back to back. I walked out to this little building they had and it was great. I just sat there, not saying a word, just listening to a couple of real coaches talk. Pat Maloney, the old Detroit outfielder, was there and guys like that. I was in my glory, you know, and yet I knew I was an outsider. They finally put Pete in to pinch-hit and I know this made Pete feel pretty good. At least they had gotten him in the game. Another time Pete came running up to where I was and he said, 'Dad, I'm going over to Dunedin to play with the Indianapolis ball club." The Reds had a working agreement with the Indiana team, too. See, all these teams had been working out at Plant Field in Tampa and the manager of the Indianapolis team had Pete's name on the starting lineup. Well, I said to him, 'Pete, don't worry about me now. You just go up there and hustle.' So he got on the charter bus they had waiting, only the manager of the Indianapolis team gets off the bus and yells over to me, 'Hey, Mr. Rose, do you want a ride over with us?' Wasn't that nice of them? All I could think of to say was, 'Gee, yes, I'd sure appreciate it if it's all right. . . .' I'll never forget that day, sitting in that bus with more than two dozen kids all dreaming of baseball, and we watched the orange groves go by. Best, when we got there, Pete played the whole game and I think Pete felt good, too. He felt they were at least looking at him and that he wasn't lost in the crowd. . . ."

My dad is really okay, isn't he?

There was another time he was down in Tampa—this was my second year in the minors—and he told a reporter about how he ran into another kid like me, just starting out. What he said pretty well sums up how it is to be young and to show up that first day at the park.

"I was walking across the bridge," my dad said, "and the son of a fellow I used to play ball with, his name was Bobby Steinbeck, just happened to be walking from the hotel to the ball park, too. They had signed this boy and two other local guys from the Cincinnati area and, of course, these kids reported later than the rest of them. It happened that the three had just got to town that day and were walking to the ball park when I ran into them. I was tickled to death. I mean, this was great. I talked to the three kids as we walked to the park and I could tell they were over-awed by everything that was happening to them. Well, we finally walked into the park itself and there were quite a few guys in uniform. You should have seen the look on Bobby Steinbeck's face. I mean, there were all these other guys out there, suited up, and really looking flashy because they had been playing ball all winter. Right then, I felt sad. I could see the discouragement on the faces of these three kids. They wondered how they ever could compete. . . ."

Yeah, I remember that moment when it happened to me. Lucky, I got the breaks. Bobby, who had been a real humdinger of a player at Elder High School—the archenemy of Western Hills High School!—wasn't as lucky. Maybe it was, as my dad said, because it was the first time some of us kids were away from home. Maybe it's because the first sight of all that hotshot competition tears them apart. Whatever it is, good guys who should make it sometimes don't make it. Bobby was released in a couple of weeks. One day he was there; the next day he wasn't. That's the kind of stuff that tears you up inside. He was every bit as good as I was—and actually he was a darned sight better—but he got his release and that, which makes me sad, is that. It is real scary going to Tampa for the first time. But it's beautiful. And then to have it not happen—well, I'm sorry. I mean it. Everybody who loves baseball and works at it deserves the best. Only sometime it just doesn't come along.

Probably the loneliest sight in the world is to see a guy who has been released, killing time at the ball park, watching the rest of us work out, while he stands there in civvies, hanging onto his suitcase, and waiting for the bus that will take him away from everything he'd ever dreamed of. When you're out on the field, you try not to look. That could be you, standing there, on the outside, looking in. And you get a gut feeling because there are no guarantees in baseball. That's him today. Tomorrow it could—for real—be you. So you practice a little harder and pretend baseball will always be there. And you know inside it won't. So you hustle harder to make the dream last.

Also, when you play in Macon, you have to avoid whatever frogs you can. See, we used to have a guy on our Macon team. He was from Venezuela and he just hated frogs, which was too bad because in Macon it rained a lot. And every time it rained, out would come the frogs. Well, one night after it rained Mel Queen was over there in right field and this guy was in center field. He didn't know that before the game Mel had got a frog and taped it to a ball. So there they were having practice throws, Mel Queen throws this ball that has a frog as a guest, and listen, Mel can throw pretty good to begin with. This guy caught the ball—and the frog—and that was all, brother. He threw away his glove and started running. It took quite awhile to get him back in the game. But, as I say, when in Macon, watch out for frogs. Or, at least, if it rains, watch out for Mel Queen.

We needed something to relieve the monotony of all that traveling—and listen, we sure used to travel a lot in the minors, especially when we were over there playing for Macon. Most of the trips were not *too* bad. From Macon to Augusta was okay. But there was one run we hated. That was a seventeen-hour trip in a station wagon from Macon to Lynchburg, Virginia. We'd travel until two or three in the afternoon, play a game that night, and hope our hotel rooms wouldn't be too darned hot. We played places like Knoxville and Atlanta, too. We knew more speed traps than the automobile club ever listed. We learned them the hard way.

For instance one time my mother and dad brought my new Corvette to Knoxville where we were playing and Dave Bristol said sure, I could run it back to Macon. I guess Bristol figured I'd be safer inside a car than on top of one, which I did once to scare the pants off the guys. What happened was, there were eight of us jammed in a station wagon, the long night haul was a drag, and there I was, piled in back on top of the equipment, so to break the monotony I sneaked the back window open. Then, when the guys weren't noticing, I climbed out the back window—while the wagon was zipping along in the sixties—and I climbed up on the roof of the wagon to ride awhile there, which was cool and good. After I did this for a while, I got bored, so I leaned down over the front windshield and waved at the driver. The poor guy almost flipped. So you can see why Dave Bristol figured it would be better for me to drive *inside* my own car rather than ride atop one of theirs. So there Helms and I were, tooling back to Macon in my Corvette, and I got so pleased with the way it was running, I passed a car in a no-passing zone somewhere in the night. All of a sudden the car I passed turned into a police car. Its driver picked up a red light he had on the seat beside him, plugged it in, and that was all, brother. There was this kangaroo court and it cost us about eighty dollars. Luckily we were close to home because that took all the cash we had. All we had between us and home was a half tank of gas.

"I don't know where you're the most trouble," Helms muttered, since I'd borrowed most of the traffic fine money from him. "Riding on top of a station wagon or in your own car. If it were not for the pleasure of your company, which is no pleasure, I'd just as soon walk."

Bristol just shook his head, chewed his tobacco, and gave me a look. Then he spit. Maybe he was thinking about the time we almost lost one of our pitchers because he happened to fall through the roof—of a hotel.

The pitcher shall be nameless in this telling of the story but on the other hand, Art Shamsky and I, since we are the souls of innocence, will identify ourselves. It seems that one hot and steamy night we were sitting around our second-floor hotel room in Augusta, wishing we were cooler. The walls of the hotel were thin. We heard—in the next room—an interesting party going on. We wanted to attend but had not been invited. So we decided to attend anyway.

"We'll just look in," the pitcher said.

"Look in?" I said. "How?"

"What we'll do," he said, "is step out on the roof. There's room enough. Then we can look in to see if the party is interesting enough to invite ourselves to."

"We're two floors up," I said.

"We got nothing else to do," the pitcher said.

That point was hard to argue with.

So we three climbed carefully through the open window onto the roof, which was just wide enough to hold us. When the three of us were out there, the pitcher made the mistake of concentrating too hard on the party. He stepped back one step too far into the gutter, which was nothing much at all. The first thing Art and I know is, our friend has dropped through the roof to the floor below. The only thing that kept him from falling completely through was he held out his arms and stopped himself. All we could see were his head and shoulders and arms.

And his unhappy expression.

He was quiet so nobody else would hear him, but he was terribly unhappy about something.

"I suppose," said Art, "we'd better pull him up. It's a long fall if he lets go."

"I suppose," I said.

I think, at that moment, the pitcher hated us. But we pulled him up anyway. We laughed so hard we almost fell off the roof ourselves. We didn't, though. Dave Bristol would have chewed us out good if we had gone and got ourselves killed. He doesn't like guys to kid around like that.

So that was pretty much what the bush leagues were back then. Some of the stuff tore your heart out and some of the stuff made you grow up fast. And lots of time you behaved like a bunch of kids on the first day of summer vacation. I spent two and a half years in that apprenticeship. It was the greatest apprenticeship a guy could have, but sooner or later every apprenticeship has to end. Besides, I was itching to play in the majors. Playing in the majors is something you can't force. You have to hustle, play your heart out, and—when nobody is looking—pray a lot. There I was in the minors, and I had improved, but I could have been dropped at any time. They don't hand you the major leagues on a silver platter.

Maybe the real turning point for me, back then, was when we'd split the team into halves every once in a while. Half would go to Mexico City to play and the other half would stay home. The tip for me was when I went to Mexico and got only two for twenty. I came back feeling mighty low. But the first game back we played Vero Beach, Florida, and Hutch stuck me right there in the starting lineup. Up to this time I had never had a major-league contract. Matter of fact, we came all the way north and played Charleston, West Virginia, and that was when I signed my contract—my major-league contract—the night before opening day. I had heard rumors from reporters that it might happen but I wasn't sure.

My dad, back at home, heard it on the radio.

I guess that was the greatest newscast he'd ever heard. At least that's what he keeps saying.

So there I was, my apprenticeship over. And there I was in Cincinnati, playing for the Reds.

I had come home.

6 When I first joined the Cincinnati Reds, Fredrick Charles Hutchinson was the manager. He was then fifty-six years old. He had started out in the majors in 1939 with Detroit and, except for service in World War Two, he was with the team till 1953. One year he had a batting average of .000, but that figures. The year was 1941 when he played in only two games, had been at bat only twice, and had to his chagrin struck out both times. The year I joined the Reds was the year Harmon Killebrew had a hot bat for Minneapolis, hitting the most home runs in the American League, forty-five in all. In the National League that year Hank Aaron led the list with forty-four home runs. That was the year Vada Pinson, batting like there was no tomorrow, got 204 hits to lead the National League. Jim Maloney's pitching percentage was .767—with 23 wins, 265 strikeouts, and 6 shutouts. Joe Nuxhall, now in the broadcast booth, gave out the fewest walks per nine innings, 1.61. Nineteen-sixty-three was a good year to join the club.

We had guys like Gordy Coleman, Frank Robinson, Johnny Edwards, and Jim Maloney. We had Freese, Cardenas, Harper, Pinson, Kasko, Skinner, Pavletich, Keough, and Spencer. For pitchers we had Maloney, as I said, as well as O'Toole, Nuxhall, Tsitouris, Jay, Purkey, Worthington, and Henry. And they had, for better or for worse, me—playing the first time in the majors. The year before, 1962, under Fred Hutchinson, the Reds had won 98 and lost 64. So Robinson started the 1963 season with a 1962 batting average of .342 to shoot at. Pinson was out to better his .292 average, Cardenas was out to topple his 1962 record of .294 —and there I stood, switch-hitting, trying to compete with all of them. I had arrived in the majors and I wanted to stay. This was where I had been heading all my life. I sure hoped that I wouldn't make hash of it.

Actually I wasn't nervous about opening day until just before the game. That's when they brought the whole Rose clan down to get some pictures. My dad was proud as thunder but I could tell he was nervous, too. My mother posed like a veteran. Then there was the umpire shouting "Play ball!" and there I was—in the majors for real.

Opening days in Cincinnati will forever be special events in my hometown. Everything seems to come to a stop but the traffic lights. But that opening day, of course, was one I'll never forget. We were playing the Pittsburgh Pirates and Earl Francis was pitching for them. He has finished the 1962 season with 9 wins and 8 losses and an earned run average of 3.07. Pittsburgh had finished fourth in 1962, one game behind the Reds. I was at second base and lead-off man.

When I got up to bat the fans cheered—not because of me but because the Reds were starting off another season. So there I stood, facing Earl Coleman Francis, who had been with Pittsburgh the two years I had been traveling around the minors. He had actually started with Pittsburgh in 1960, the first year having an average of 1.000 because he had only pitched in one game and had the good fortune to win that. In 1961 his percentage dropped to .200, winning 2 and losing 8. Anyway, there I stood facing the six foot two, 210-pound pitcher the stork had delivered in 1936 to a fine place called Slab Fork, West Virginia.

The first pitch—nothing. But, as I had done ever since I had been a runny-nosed kid in the Knot Hole circuit, I followed the ball from the moment it left the pitcher's hand until it plopped—with a thud—into the catcher's glove.

Unfortunately, Jocko Conlan, the plate umpire, thought I had been looking back at the ball to dispute the call. The first thing a major-league umpire ever said to me was what Jocko growled at me that day after that first pitch.

"Listen, you young rookie, don't look back here at me. I don't need no help with my calls."

Did I offer a comment back to him? Listen, are you kidding? I didn't do anything. I was too scared to do anything. There were 30,000 fans up there in the stands, watching. I just stood there, waiting and hoping and praying.

The next pitch came at me.

"Ball," the umpire said.

The third pitch was the same.

By this time, though, I think Mr. Conlan got the idea that I wasn't trying to help him in the pursuit of his chosen profession. I guess he figured that's the way the rookie was going to be, keeping his eye on the ball. Later he told me that he was sure puzzled that first time I was at bat. By then, though, we knew each other well enough to laugh about it. Not that first game, though. Listen, that first game was no laughing matter to me.

The pitcher wound up—and hurled another bad pitch.

"Ball!" the umpire said.

So there I was, the lead-off batter for the Reds that season, and I had drawn a walk on four straight pitches. I took off for first base like a bird.

That was the first time the hometown fans had seen the way I had been hustling all my life. I didn't walk to first. I didn't stroll. I scooted as if my life depended on it. And there I stood, on first, listening to the way the fans reacted. There was one big cheer. And it was real good to hear that.

Well, I stood there on first and pretty soon Frank Robinson slugged himself a beautiful home run so I went chugging around the bags ahead of him, and there I was, scoring the first run of the season. That was a real good feeling, too. I'll never forget waiting there at home plate for Frank to come in. It was like being a bit player in the greatest movie ever made.

The rest of that first game is a kind of blur. That was the day I went 0 for 3, plus that first-inning walk. We did beat the Pirates, though, if that helps and to me it sure does. I helped out in four double plays. On the other hand I wasn't exactly the greatest star the Reds had that first day because Bob Skinner, who had been with Pittsburgh ever since I was ten years old, came to the plate (he had hit .302 the year before) and slammed a ball at me. Only instead of getting my meathooks on it the ball sailed through my legs, which embarrassed not only me but my dad up there in the stands. When the first game was over I really didn't have too much to show off about because the run I had scored I had got on a walk and it took Frank Robinson to bring me in. But still it was good being in the locker room after the game. I felt, for the first time, that I had arrived.

It wasn't until the next day that I got my first major-league hit and I guess a guy will always remember his first one or he shouldn't be in the game to begin with. It was off the guy they call the Warrior, Bob Friend. He had been with Pittsburgh since 1951 and the year before, 1962, he had won 17 and lost 16 and had pitched five shutouts. I really creamed that ball and then I really hustled to make it a triple. I was proud as a peacock standing there on third, dusting myself off. It had been a solid hit straight down the left-field aisle. A beauty. I felt good starting off with a triple because in the minors I got triples just about every time I spit. But there is a big difference between getting a triple in the minors and getting one off that six-foot Hoosier from La Fayette. There's as much difference between major- and minor-league pitching as there is between day and night.

What I mean is, in the majors you can count on getting good pitchers hurling at you every day. So you get accustomed to it and you expect it. I was glad I didn't expect it those first few games or the pitching would have scared the pants off me. But there I stood, on third base, and I was on cloud nine.

And then, there we were, on the road. I was seeing ball parks I had only read about before. I was seeing cities that I had only seen in the movies before. That first year on the road was really something. Each city was a new experience. The first thing I would do is go out and stare at each ball park. I was familiar with Cincinnati's but as far as these others were concerned, I was a stranger. Back then, New York was in the old park, the Polo Grounds. And St. Louis was still in the old Sportsman's Park. But Los Angeles and San

Francisco were shiny new. Houston was still the old park, filled with mosquitoes. Mosquitoville. That's what we guys called that old Houston place. Some parks I didn't like then and I don't like now. Like Candlestick Park. Listen, it's cold out there. The place holds 42,500 and I'll bet you lots of times they're all huddled together trying to get warm, and wishing the fog would go away. San Francisco is a pretty town but it sure is a damp and chilly place to play baseball, which I personally like to consider a hot-weather game. Also, Candlestick Park has a rough infield. Don't forget that.

The places I really like to play in? Well, believe it or not, there's Chicago. When those bleacher bums in Wrigley Field get on me, they forget one thing. That kind of stuff only makes me work harder. So, in reality, they aren't getting my goat. They're getting the best I got in me. The worst thing that crowd ever threw at me was a crutch, a legitimate crutch! Listen, I was playing there one day when they had to call the game for a few minutes so the groundskeepers could clear off the field. They had thrown everything my way. They had thrown those paper cups for beer, popcorn boxes, hot dogs, fish, and even chicken bones. When they got through throwing stuff my way the field looked like an incinerator. I got the biggest kick out of those characters in the Wrigley Field bleachers. I can't get mad at them. How can I? They take their baseball as seriously as I take my baseball which make them, whether they want to be or not, my kind of people.

Los Angeles is a great place to play baseball. Their field is actually beautiful. I'd rate them second to Chicago as the best place to play away games. Then, there's Philadelphia. That's a good baseball town.

And add the Houston fans and their Astrodome. But the prettiest park of them all is in San Diego. Then, there's St. Louis. Listen, that stadium they got there is a real humdinger. What I suppose I'm saying is, in one way or the other, I like to play in most of the parks. The only two that really bug me, and it's not their fault, are San Francisco which I told you about, and Montreal. I mean, I keep saying baseball is supposed to be played where it's warm. Right? But in Montreal you got to go out there in your long underwear. A player just can't loosen up. Some guys dig those places. Willie Mays likes them. But I don't. Oh, and add Atlanta to the places I like to play. It's really going to be a humdinger of a place this season when they get that Astroturf on it.

Personally Crosley Field, field-wise, is about as good a place to play baseball as any you could name. And isn't the new riverfront park going to be something! Good infield. Good outfield. Good background. The new park here in Cincinnati is going to be out of sight! I'm sure going to hate to leave Crosley Field. I did a lot of growing up there in that old park. But I am looking forward to the first game down there by the river.

My first trip to New York City impressed me. They had us down there in the Hotel Roosevelt, which is a long way from the park so we'd go to the park by chartered bus. I saw more bridges than any city ought to have. And I'd spend the whole bus ride with my nose pressed against the window, gawking out at the people. Listen, some of them were real freaks. They wouldn't have lasted ten seconds in Sedamsville. We used to go through Harlem on the way to the Polo Grounds and that always struck me as kind of sad. Seems like there was nothing but acres and acres of tenements, each one in worse shape than the others. We'd yell at the people and they'd yell back at us. Nothing mean. Nobody was mad at anyone. And I remember one time we were traveling through some pretty ritzy neighborhood where we had seen people walking their dogs and cats on a leash, only there was this one guy and on his leash was a duck! Yeah, New York is a lot different than Sedamsville.

Back then, in the beginning, I used to take along two suits for a ten-day road trip. Now I take along at least ten. But there was a reason I didn't lug so many around those first years. I only had two suits.

One of my first roommates on the road was Daryl Spencer, who had come to Cincinnati by way of Los Angeles, St. Louis, San Francisco, and New York. He was older than I was. He had been with the New York team, batting .294, when I was down there in the Knot Hole circuit. A real nice guy from Wichita, they called him the Big Dee and listen, that guy had plenty of baseball savvy. I think that's why Hutch made us roommates. Hutch was hoping some of Spencer's wisdom would rub off on me. We used to sit around the hotels, talking nothing but baseball. What that guy didn't know about the game hadn't happened yet. If we weren't doing that when we were in New York, I would be down to the train station, during rush hour, watching all the bodies go by. The commuter crowds sure were big. I went once to see the Empire State Building, too, but I guess I'm not the true sightseer. I never saw the Staten Island Ferry. I never walked along Broadway and Times Square. I never did much of anything.

The way I figure things is, if I go out and *walk* all day, rubbernecking, I'm going to be pooped. I figure I should save my energy for the game of baseball, which is why I'm there and why they're paying me. So mostly, in these towns on road trips, I'd hardly leave the hotel room. If I had my way, I'd have eaten all my meals there, too. If we had a night game in New York, for instance, I'd go down to the lobby around five and wait for the 5:30 game bus. I hate being late. And I hate missing buses. Anyway, in those days, who wanted to miss the bus from downtown Manhattan to the Polo Grounds? That's a cab ride I just couldn't afford.

In Chicago I walked around a little. And I used to go to picture shows a lot. I'm not what you'd call a very big drinker so I couldn't spend my time sitting around bars, could I? And when I was single I used to keep the eye out for the stewardesses on the flights. I'm human. And I'd go down to Rush Street. Also, I remember one night I went to a place that had a Greek belly dancer. She would have made a dandy shortstop.

The first game away from Cincinnati, though, was Philadelphia. Art Mahaffey, who had gone to Western Hills High School long before I had, was pitching for the Phillies. He had been there since 1960, and in 1962 he had won 19 and lost 14, including 1 shutout; only the chilly day I faced him, he was hot and struck me out four straight times. That was when Art threw real good. So I'll never forget my *first* road game. I wish I could though. That was a real cold night we played, the temperature was 32 degrees, and there we were, all huddled together in the park, and the pitcher was making a monkey out of me.

A lot of guys tried to make a monkey out of me that first year because they figured I was young and immature—and most of the times they figured right. At least I didn't have any superstitions like some players did. Sammy Ellis, for instance, when he finishes his stint on the pitching mound, will never walk straight to the dugout. He refuses to step on the infield grass. He goes the long way, out there to the dirt, and walks in. When I came to the Reds, he had already been with the team one year, winning 2 and losing 2. The first year I was there, which was 1963, he wasn't there, but he was in 1964, winning 10 and losing 3. Anyway, as I was saying, he kept off the infield grass a lot. Meanwhile guys were trying to bug me into doing dumb things.

Like one time I was batting and I forget who was catching, but this was when I got caught running that red light in Newport, Kentucky, and the catcher, all the time I was batting, was saying, "Hey, Pete, what were you really doing over there?"

"Nothing," I would tell him—and zip, there would go the ball.

"Are you sure?"

"I wasn't doing anything over there."

Zip! There went the ball again.

I suppose, though, the craziest conversation there ever was between a batter and a catcher was in one game against Philadelphia. Mike Ryan was catching. There he was, hunched behind the plate, and he was saying, "Now, Pete, I'm going to tell you what's coming next."

I paid no attention to him.

"Here comes a fast ball," he said, "Here comes a fast ball!"

And sure enough, there came a fast ball.

I said, "Aw, shut up, man. I don't want to know what's coming."

"Here comes a curve."

Sure enough. It was a curve.

"Listen," I said to plate umpire Doug Harvey, "Can you shut this guy up?"

"Not me," said the umpire. "I can't shut him up."

"Here comes another fast ball."

And it was.

And would you believe it, he got me out two straight times.

When I came to bat the third time there was a guy on second, Mike called the way the ball was coming, and I creamed the thing, hitting a double.

Well, the next day he didn't call any more pitches when I was batting. He seemed sad about something.

But ballplayers are always talking together out there during the game. Like, when I get on first and there's Deron Johnson, who was with the Reds from 1964 to 1967. We'll talk because he used to live in the apartment right under ours and I ask him about his kids and he asks me about mine. Also, if you're playing second, you keep talking to the runner so he stays close by and doesn't go strolling off to third the moment your back is turned. But sometimes they'll catch you and there you'll stand with egg on your face.

Maury Wills—Maurice Morning Wills, if you please!—who played for Los Angeles and then Pittsburgh is a wise old owl who once almost caught me. I had just done one of my fancy headfirst slides into second and was standing on the bag, dusting myself off, when he says, "Excuse me, Pete. I'm going to kick off the bag."

He said that thinking a guy would automatically step off the bag, which would be a natural reaction, but I got one foot off the bag and I stopped.

"No," I said, "I don't think I'll do it at the moment."

Because he was standing there, holding the ball.

I did that to a guy once, though. He slid into second, raised a powerful cloud of dust, and I said, "Lemme kick off the bag, will you?"

"Sure," the guy said—and I tagged him and he was

out! It can be very embarrassing, so I'd rather it happen to the other guy. Tommy Helms tricked a guy out on third like that once.

I was having fun that first year and I was working hard, too. The more games I played the more I learned. But a guy doesn't get baseball wisdom in one season. Like, it takes a while to know when you can stretch a single into a double. Make it and the fans love you. Blow it and they call you a hotdog. But you have to make up your mind fast. You have to think of a bunch of things, all at once, like who is the outfielder going after the ball, the thickness of the grass out there, and if there are two outs you've got everything to gain and nothing to lose. What's the good of me holing up on first base? I'm not the best base stealer in the world and everybody out there knows it. But if I make it to second, whoever bats behind me has only to get a single and on I go. If I get put out, look at it this way. That means we got a good second or third hitter leading off the next inning. A lot of things like that enter into whether you keep going or not. But I don't get thrown out that much. I've never got thrown out with no outs. I usually try for that second base when there are two outs. But look at it this way. A single can score you no matter what base you're on. Anyway, I'm just as useful on first because that holds the first baseman on and leaves a big hole for a left-handed pull hitter to aim at. There's a lot more to baseball than just swinging away. But what the fans dig most, I guess, are those headfirst slides I do.

"Why slide head first?" That's what they're always asking me.

Well, listen, that's the only way to do it, that's why. When you slide head first your momentum doesn't slow—in fact you actually pick up momentum—and slides are a matter of inches per second. Also, I can see what's going on. Slide in on my fanny and all I see is the sky, which isn't too helpful. On the other hand, you'll not find me making too many headfirst slides into home. I did that once and almost got cut to pieces by the catcher's shin guard. No, I wouldn't recommend sliding into home. But out there on the field, I never get spiked. Or, at least I haven't so far. A guy sliding seldom will because of the way the guys are covering the base. The baseman is usually straddling the base. His feet aren't on it. Oh, if he jumps up sometimes you might be in bad shape, but it's easier to get a broken ankle than it is to get a broken hand. Another thing, when you slide headfirst you might see the ball go by third and off you go. But if you slide the other way, you don't stand a chance. You have to waste time looking for a signal from the coach.

Some fields are better to slide headfirst on than others, though. Pittsburgh is the roughest place of all. The ground is so hard you get your elbows and your knees messed up. Actually, your elbows and knees are all that ever take the beating because your stomach acts as a cushion.

Now that first year I played in 157 games and I went to the plate 623 times. That first year I got 25 doubles, 9 triples, and much to my surprise, half a dozen home runs. I just don't consider myself a home-run hitter, I guess, and the statistics will bear me out. Also that first year I struck out 72 times and walked 55 times. Once out there on the bases, I managed to steal 13 times—successfully, that is. I played the 157 games at second base, missing only 5 games. I think the opposing pitchers that first year booked me as a good curve-ball hitter, so they were always trying to jam me with one. That means they would try to slip one in there fast and on the inside. Gaylord Perry—bless him and his darned spitball!—had yet to come along, but I faced some mean and hot pitchers that first year I was in the majors. There was Sandy Koufax, who ended the 1963 season with a winning percentage of .833. Warren Spahn in Milwaukee made me earn my money, too. He ended the season with a winning percentage of .767. And add to the list of troublemakers guys like Los Angeles' Ron Perranoski, who led the league with his winning percentage of .842 (he won 16 and he lost 3); and Juan Marichal, who hailed from the Dominican Republic and who had a winning percentage that year of .758 for San Francisco. Also in 1963 he pitched a no-hitter against Houston, which didn't set too well with Houston, of course, because no-hitters always make the losing team feel blue about something.

I gained wisdom at that plate. I had to start fresh, learning to "read" every pitcher the National League had. Stuff my dad taught me helped a lot. I'd watch the pitcher and the ball practically from the moment he strolled onto the rubber till he went into the showers after the game. I think I had a pretty good eye; like, I could always tell a curve ball. What I mean is, a batter has got to be able to tell what it is the minute —*that split second*—the ball leaves the pitcher's hand. You got to know—fast—what is coming at you: curve ball, screwball, or the kitchen sink. Now when I faced Sandy Koufax that year I knew I always faced trouble. He was hot and I was young. He had pitched a no-hitter against New York the season before. And in the 1963 season he pitched a no-hitter against San Francisco. He won 25 games that year and lost only 5. He won some of them off eager-beaver rookies like me.

Like, he can throw good and hard; and frankly I think he's one of the greatest pitchers that ever lived. He was starting his ninth year in the majors when I was out there for the first time. And he had two World Series under his belt. And there I'd be, facing him, waiting for him to lay that fast ball on me—only you know how he used to get me out? He used to get me out on fork balls. I guess I'm one of the few guys he ever threw fork balls to. He'd strike me out and then he'd stand out there on the mound, laughing at me. He got the biggest kick out of doing me that way. But nobody got mad because that's the way baseball is.

But as for hating pitchers, no. I feel if a hitter is in the groove, if he's swinging his bat good, God could be out there pitching and the batter would still land a solid one. Then again, maybe the following week, the batter isn't grooving and anybody can get him out. Sometimes a knuckle-ball or a screwball pitcher will get me going into a slump because when they pitch that way they got me lunging at the ball. Slumps are funny things. You can be hitting .400 and go into a slump, just like that. I think, though, most slumps are psychological. Guys start *thinking* they're in a slump and pretty soon they are because they actually thought themselves into one. But you just got to remember that sometime in the season you're going 0 for 8 or 0 for 10. Whether you want to or not, you will anyway. Very few players bat 1.000.

"Watch the other guys," that's the advice they hammered at me my first year in the majors. "Watch how the other guys do it, Pete, and you might pick up a few new tricks."

I looked a lot that first season and I still look. Like, I spent the first year at second base and I was always watching how the other teams worked out practicing their double plays. And I was always doing it, too. Practicing, practicing, practicing. Nobody can ever get enough practice. Especially nobody can ever get enough practice at ground balls. A guy like Bill Mazeroski of Pittsburgh is a real beauty to watch at practice. I'd just go and stand and watch him take ground balls. He made it look so easy that he used to make me feel stupid. He's great. He's the nicest guy you'd ever want to meet, but out there, gobbling up ground balls, he's a human vacuum cleaner. After watching him I suit up and there I'd be, struggling to do what he did so well.

"Come on now, Pete," he used to tell me. "This is the way you got to go about it. . . ."

And he would tell me how to relax my hands and stuff like that because that's the wonderful guy he is. He wasn't selfish. He was baseball-minded enough to want to help a squirt like me, even though I was on the other team. I really appreciated that guy. He had been with Pittsburgh since 1956, holding down the fort at second base, and he was always in there, helping rookies like me. There's a lot of beautiful stuff like that going on in baseball. Back then, in the majors, we used to be able to go out and stand behind the batting cage and watch guys bat but they don't let you do that anymore. They call it fraternizing—like fraternizing with the enemy, I suppose, because they feel the public doesn't like to see two teams saying hellos to one another. Now we can't even talk to a guy on another team without getting fined twenty-five dollars, and that's the way baseball is, too.

Well, I had fun that first year, but the Reds ended in fifth place anyway, 13 games behind Los Angeles, because we had won 86 and we had lost 76, giving us a percentage of .531, which was not enough. We had scored 648 runs that year while our opponents had scored only 578 runs against us. We had been good but not good enough.

"Wait till next year," was the cry, but that's the way things are. The next year—1964—was my sophomore year in the majors. And, if you remember how I messed up my tenth grade at Western Hills High School, you know what a lousy sophomore I make. My luck held true. My bad luck, that is. I had finished my first year and was waiting for the second, where I would almost end up out of the majors for keeps.

But first, there was this thing called the military. Uncle Sam had optioned me.

7 After I had been to bat 623 times in the major leagues they sent me off to play in another kind of game, the one called the military. In other words, Peter Edward Rose went to Fort Knox, Kentucky, on the waivers every guy has got, and there I was, standing around with about five dozen other recruits, wondering if the army life was all it was cut out to be. Listen, that was a chilling day, standing out there in our civvies, while everybody else was running around in uniform and looking like they know the score. Heck, back then we didn't even know what the game was. That's what raw material we were.

But I'm not complaining. Listen, doesn't every guy go through the same thing?

That was the year Koufax struck out fifteen batters to set some new kind of World Series record, so that National League via the Los Angeles team beat the New York Yankees four straight games. That was also the World Series where Drysdale pitched a shutout, allowing only three hits, and walking only one batter. But none of this helped us as we stood there in the recruit depot. The New York Yankees were taken taken down a peg and so were we. And we had no umpire around to give us the benefit of a disputed call. All we had was a bunch of corporals and sergeants who, when we first saw them, seemed very angry about something. But we learned later this is the natural stance of a drill instructor. After the Angels gave the Giants a hard time, the drill instructors were braying instructions at us in machine-gun paragraphs none of us could understand, but we stood around, listening anyway, because that's the way recruits are the world over, isn't it?

To make matters worse our company officer, the guy in charge of our recruit platoon, was a West Point second lieutenant who was a little guy and also he didn't care too much for jockstraps, which is what he labeled professional athletes. I tried to be nice to the guy but since I was a National Guardsman and he was a career soldier, the two of us never quite got off on the right foot. No sweat, though. He had his good points, which I looked hard to find and eventually I found some. The other officers and noncoms and the guys who were my fellow recruits were a fine bunch. I wasn't a baseball player there. I was just one of the guys. That's the way I wanted it and so it was okay. Besides, I had no airs to put on. Some of the guys in our platoon could run rings around me as far as brains were concerned. And we were all in the same mess together. That's the way we looked at it. Since everybody felt that way, we actually had some fun. But on the other hand only a nut would admit that being a recruit is a barrel of laughs. It's a barrel of something, though. Another recruit said that, mother. I didn't.

So there we were, standing around, and there was our platoon leader. He was Sergeant Robert E. Lee— and I suppose he was from the South. He acted as if he was a mean son of a buck but that was before we got better acquainted.

He put his hands on his hips and bellowed, "All right! Which one of you guys is Rose?"

Since none of the other guys said anything, I figured he was talking to me and that I was really in for it.

"I am," I said.

He looked a look that was a combination of all the mean looks umpires ever looked.

"You mean," he shouted, *"I am, sir."*

"I am . . . sir!" I said.

"All right," he shouted. "What I want is for you to be my platoon sergeant. I figure that anybody that can play major-league baseball might have enough brains to be the platoon guide. Right?"

"Right," I said.

"Right, sir!" he bellowed and that was that.

I was glad that happened because I learned real fast that it meant when the rest of the platoon was standing around at attention, not able to scratch where it itched, I had to walk around like I was some kind of leader, which we all knew I certainly was not. The other guys in the platoon didn't mind that I had got the position because we were all in the same boat. I was always one of the guys because I didn't know how to be anything else. We heard later that some of the recruit leaders of some of the other recruit platoons let the sudden "rank" go to their heads and went around playing high and mighty. Funny how a title will affect some guys, isn't it? All I wanted to do was keep my nose clean. I wasn't about to become the Great American Recruit Platoon Leader. I liked the guys in our recruit platoon too much to play that dumb game with them.

A reporter asked me once if it was easier or rougher in basic training because I was Pete Rose the Ballplayer. Well, I answered him that it would have been rougher but I was with a platoon of pretty good guys. And as platoon leader I didn't win any prizes for our platoon. I got us through just what we had to get through—and that was all. There were four platoons in our recruit company. The others always passed inspection better than ours. We never did pass an inspection with flying colors. Does that show what kind of platoon leader I was? I was too busy being one of the guys and goofing off with the rest of them.

On the other hand, at the end of basic training they give these guys this test, where everything we learned is tested, and if we pass, we pass, and if we fail, the guy has to go through basic training all over again. I am kind of proud to say that every guy in our platoon passed that test. We were the only platoon that didn't have to flunk a recruit, which I think is pretty good. So you can't say our platoon was a load of dumbheads. Still, every time there was an inspection, our platoon ranked last. I guess we just weren't good at dusting.

"So we don't win any blue ribbons at inspection," one of the guys said after we had been eaten out for about the fiftieth time. "Look at the bright side."

"Like what?" I said.

"Like the platoon that rates lowest in inspection gets to eat last and like our platoon always has to be food servers, which really ain't so bad. That way our platoon gets extra food and the best of it. I mean, look at the bright side. The other slobs have to eat what we don't want. We save the real goodies for our platoon."

As you can see, our platoon was always in there— thinking—*and* eating. You wouldn't exactly call it the Good Life but it was better than being with some of those other platoons.

How many guys were there altogether in the platoon I was in? There were seventy-four of them. A few were from Cincinnati but most were from Chicago. None of the guys in my platoon admitted to sitting in the bleachers, though, at Wrigley Field and throwing stuff at me. So life wasn't so awfully bad there.

Being a baseball player *did* have some advantages. Like, the day we marched over to the barber shop to get ourselves sheared. They are supposed to shave us bald, you know, only in addition to doing everything the other recruits were doing, I was supposed to go into Louisville with this colonel one night for a sports banquet, so I guess the army didn't want the civvies to see my shiny dome.

I was standing there in the barber shop, getting more and more depressed, watching guys sit in the chair and watching the barbers hack away. I made up my mind to one thing. The guy who did my hair was one barber I was never going to tip.

Only the colonel was standing around, too, and he sidles up to the barber and said, "See that guy over there?" He indicates me.

"Yeah," said the barber who, being a civilian, didn't have to go around saying "sir" to everything that moved.

"Well," said the colonel, "that's Pete Rose from the Cincinnati Reds."

"How about that?" said the barber.

"And the rest of the recruits are waiting to see Pete's flattop get the works," the colonel said.

"How about that?" said the barber.

So far, during the conversation, he had ripped through two enforced customers, which gives you an idea of the care the barber went around lavishing on us recruits.

"You're going to have to do the army a favor," the colonel said. "I've got Pete scheduled for a sports banquet in town and I would hate to see him looking like some of your other customers."

"Sure," said the barber, but I guess he wasn't too happy. Hacking away at uncomplaining recruits must have robbed him of his talents. Maybe he wasn't sure he had any haircutting talents left. Still, to him, a colonel was a colonel and he wasn't about to rock the boat.

He cut my hair nice—short—but nice. But I could tell he wasn't pleased about doing it. Barbers who cut recruits must have a special code of honor that says if the recruit looks halfway decent after getting up from the barber chair, the barber will be drummed out of the trade.

I'll be honest. That was one monent the guys in my platoon didn't exactly look upon me with favor. I don't blame them either. If I had been them, running around bald, I would have been unhappy, too, at anybody who beat the tonsorial rap. They didn't stay unhappy long. But they were running around kind of uncool with me until some of their own hair got going again.

Most of the time we were all too busy goofing off and horsing around to get mad at one another. We were, as a platoon, all against Robert E. Lee, our platoon sergeant, and like recruits will do everywhere, any time we could give him a hard time and get away with it, you can bet your bottom dollar that we did.

Like I used to get the biggest kick out of upsetting the sergeant, especially in the area of military etiquette, which was a subject I never won any prizes in. Take the time, right after the trip to the barber shop, that this colonel took me down to Louisville to this banquet when the army was showing me off. Now this colonel was a real nice guy, recruit stuff didn't bug him because he was way up there beyond that jazz, and going and coming we had a good time. I was the kid fresh from the Cincinnati Reds and he was the baseball fan. We got along fine. And there we were, driving back into my recruit area at Fort Knox, just as Sergeant Robert E. Lee was lining up our platoon for its evening formation.

When he saw the colonel's car pull up, the sergeant bellowed "Attention!" and made sure everybody was, including himself, because you know how recruit sergeants get a large charge out of things of that nature.

I looked out as the car drove up and I saw that the second lieutenant in charge of us was there, too, ramrod straight, real West Point. Everything was silent. You could hear a pin drop.

Well, I opened the car door, got out, leaned back in the car, and said, "Hey, thanks, colonel. I'll see you later, old buddy."

The car drove off. Now, the colonel wasn't mad. He was a real good guy. But as I walked over to where my platoon was, you should have seen the look on the face of that second lieutenant. I won't even tell you about the look on the sergeant's face. You wouldn't sleep nights. What I'm saying is, these two were not exactly pleased with the way I did military etiquette things, like an enlisted man is supposed to salute an officer when they part, and like it isn't exactly regulation for a recruit to go around calling a colonel "old buddy."

"Rose!" called the lieutenant after the colonel's car had gone.

"Yes, sir," I said.

He glared.

"Why didn't you salute that colonel?" he said. He was seething.

"Well," I said, "I don't really know why I didn't, lieutenant, sir. What I mean is, we've been together most of the afternoon. And he's my friend. Like he's my buddy, sir."

The platoon, still at attention, got the biggest kick out of that. But on the other hand, the lieutenant didn't. I guess that's the way lieutenants are, though. That's why I later became a cook instead of an officer. I wasn't exactly officer material.

Then there was the time we gave Sergeant Robert E. Lee a real hard time. I remember that one night me and another guy hid the sergeant's Volkswagen. Actually, we didn't exactly hide it. First we "borrowed" it when he wasn't looking and we drove it around. *Then* we hid it. We let the poor guy suffer, thinking it was gone for good, and just as he was about to call the military police—or the Pentagon, I'm not sure which because he was real upset—we told him where we had "seen" it.

And I was all the time sneaking down to the PX, loading up on food we weren't supposed to have, and we'd store this food like pack rats up in that crawl area above our barrack's ceiling. Only one night when the sergeant inspected up there and found we had enough food to hold out a month, he got real mad, and that ended our private stores. We had to admit that he was hard to fool. Everything—well, most everything —we thought up, some other recruit platoon long before we got there had also thought up and tried. I'm surprised the sergeant managed to keep his good nature most of the time the way he did—most of the time.

When it came to soldiering, I was a better baseball

player. I'll be the first to admit that, although the rest of the guys in the platoon will agree so fast that your head will swim. Like this business of making the "military" bed, you know, tight corners, pillow just so, blanket just so, everything trim and nice. Well, I never really mastered tucking the blanket in the way the other guys did, so I did the next best thing. I made my bed only when new sheets were issued. The rest of the time, I slept on top of my well-made bed, being careful not to turn and toss too much or it would be messed up again. I went through basic training that way, sacked out, but never in the sack. I think it is a good thing my bunk was near the heater. I might have frozen to death.

Then there was the time me and this other soldier were sitting in the john after lights out and this other guy was smoking, which he wasn't supposed to be doing—and in walked the sergeant. The other guy threw his cigarette into the toilet fast, but he wasn't fast enough for Sergeant Robert E. Lee.

"All right, all right!" the sergeant bellowed. "I see you. I see what you did. I really got you this time."

"What do you mean," I said, "when you say you got me?"

"You both were smoking cigarettes, weren't you?"

"Not us," I said.

"He wasn't," the other recruit said, "and I wasn't, either."

The sergeant pointed to the toilet bowl and bellowed, "Look! See! It's right in there!"

The other guy and I started laughing. We couldn't help ourselves. It was a riot. Listen, that sergeant was more than a mother to us.

"All I know," the sergeant said, "the smoking lamp is out."

And out the door he stomped.

Real G. I.

But don't get me wrong. After we got to know the guy we discovered he was all heart. But he was the typical sergeant, whose bark was worse than his bite. He was good for the army and good for the recruits in basic training. But we still got the biggest kick out of him.

As a leader of men I didn't win any prizes, but as followers of their dumb leader—which was me—our platoon sure had faith, even though it was terribly misplaced. There was the time I was marching our platoon somewhere in the recruit area and every time we came to a road crossing, of course, I got the road blocks out so they could stop the traffic. Well, there I was, going along, having a ball calling cadence, and I was supposed to shout, "Right flank . . . march!" only I was daydreaming so I shouted "Left flank . . . march!" instead. So there the entire platoon went, marching off the road, down the culvert, and just as they were about to straggle through a mud-filled ditch, I shouted, "Halt!" The second lieutenant was pretty mad at me for getting the platoon so much off course because I guess things like that never happened much at West Point where he learned his army things. But I was sure proud of those guys in the platoon. And they were sure proud of me, I guess, because I had said "Halt" before they went wading.

"Two seconds later, though," one of the guys said, "and we would have been hating your guts, Pete."

So somehow or other, we all managed to get out of basic and, as I say, our platoon had some real smart guys in it because none of them got held over and had to go through the whole thing again.

The most interesting day I had as a recruit? Well,

that would be the day I was there in the barracks, scrubbing the floor like there was no tomorrow. The telephone starts ringing off the wall from Cincinnati. Everybody was calling me because I had been named baseball Rookie of the Year.

"What are you going to do to celebrate?" one of the callers asked.

"Finish scrubbing the floor," I said. "There's half of it left to do."

I might have been Rookie of the Year to the baseball writers but to the army I was plain old Peter Edward Rose, private, and my job to aid the war effort was making sure that floor was scrubbed. I didn't mind, though. Other guys in the platoon got the same chores. I was no better than any of them, was I? Some of those guys were pretty darned smart. I learned a lot of things from them. From the army, I learned a lot of things, too. Mostly I learned how to scrub floors good and—with a little practice—how *not* to march a platoon into a ditch. Listen, stuff like that is pretty important in the army.

Well, after basic, I was a holdover at Fort Knox for a couple of weeks so I helped Sergeant Robert E. Lee with the next platoon, which I *didn't* march into a ditch. I wasn't real bossy or anything, which was why, I suppose, I wasn't cut out to help with recruits. I was on their side. I had just been through what they were going through and I knew exactly how they felt. Then the colonel got me a job helping the sergeant who was the baseball coach for the base. He was a funny guy. He used to let me get off every afternoon around one so I could practice basketball. Basketball keeps me in shape. Well, every morning at 7:30 I had to show up at his place to get the fire started so it would be warm when he got there. After I got the fire going, I spent the rest of the time answering the telephone. And, to break the monotony, I'd eat doughnuts and drink coffee with a captain who dropped in all the time. That was what I call the hard life.

Never went into Louisville, though, the way a lot of the guys did. Whenever I cut out, I cut out for Cincinnati. I had good reason, too. My wife, then my fiancée, was in Cincinnati. And sometimes she would drive down to Louisville, bringing cookies for the guys, and that was a big hit. We got married that weekend after I got out of basic training. I graduated from basic January 18 and got married January 25. We spent our honeymoon in a motel near Fort Knox. It wasn't exactly the greatest motel in the world. The bridal suite —which was the same as any other room in the dump —cost four bucks a night. But it had four walls, a ceiling, a television, and a roof. Some honeymoon!

Once I remember my wife brought my car down and we drove like rabbits back to Cincinnati so I could do a television commercial for Rubel Rye Bread. Well, we were really streaking up the road between Louisville and Cincinnati and we happened to pass a couple of ballplayers who were heading the other way for spring training. They said the way I was driving and the way my hair was that I looked like Clutch Cargo.

Sometimes my wife would sneak onto the base and bring my civvies. She would con the night guard (I'd better not name *him!*) and say, "Give these to Pete, will you?" So he'd give me the clothes, I'd climb in the civvies, and drive out through the front gate big as life. There were actually no gates, but you get the idea.

After basic training I got with a reserve engineering unit that was stationed in Fort Thomas, Kentucky, right across the river from Cincinnati. Bob Kennedy in that outfit was great to me. Oh, he didn't show me any favoritism because I was a ballplayer. He was great with all the guys. He would stick his neck out for us lots of times, letting us make up the drills we missed. Like when I would be on the road for the Reds there would naturally be drills that I would miss. That was okay with him so long as I made up every one of the missed drills. Yeah, he had class and he took good care of his units and us guys who were in it. The rest of the guys and I really knocked ourselves out for Kennedy because we all wanted to make him look good. I sure hope that we succeeded.

He used to take a lot of guff because of me, though. I was sorry about that stuff. Sometimes some outsiders would get upset because when I was on the road with the team I missed a drill. They didn't care that I made every one of them up again. They would quarrel if I wasn't there or if Johnny Bench wasn't there. He would try to explain how we were doing, but you know how some people are: that was never good enough for them. Like, people would write him moaning that I wasn't going to summer camp until after the regular baseball season. They'd write and complain that if their son had to go, I should have to go, too. And they were right. I don't quarrel with them for that. I went. I put in my time—no more, no less—like any of the other guys. But there were always some people ready to put you down because you happen to be a ballplayer.

The Coke machine bit was the time that made me a little mad. I was talking to this reporter about how life was in the military and I was kidding him, like nobody was allowed to take a break and have a Coke. So I said, kiddingly, there I was, guarding the Coke machine, which, funny as it seems, I really was. Only it comes out in the paper as if I'm sour on being in the unit and I'm wasting my time, sitting there with an empty weapon, guarding the Coke machine. The readers didn't know I was kidding the way the reporter wrote it. That kind of stuff bothers me. But happily for me, that kind of stuff is the exception. Most of the newspapermen I know are great. They've gone out of their way to be fair with me. You couldn't ask for a nicer bunch of guys. They love baseball as much—or more—than most players. So if one reporter puts me down I really have no right to complain. They all aren't aces but most of them are. The same is true with players. Not all of us would win Bibles.

Mostly, at the beginning, I would do my drills out on Seymour Avenue at the armory. I drilled there for a couple of years, only they changed their pattern. Instead of having weekend drills and three weekly drills a month, they stepped up the schedule from forty-two to seventy-two drills a year—and as a baseball player, listen, I just couldn't swing that kind of schedule. So they were nice enough to transfer me over the river to Fort Thomas and Bob Kennedy.

What was I over there? This may scare you to death but I was the company cook! I'm great at frying chicken or steak. And one day I made dessert, but something strange happened so I never made dessert again. Cooking for the military isn't the hardest job they got in the world. Everything is spelled out in the military cookbook. Having 120 guys sit down to dinner that I had to cook never bothered me. It may have bothered them, though, but they were kind enough not to say anything if it did. The *quantities* used to interest me. Like making iced tea, for instance.

Listen, I wish this book had ten million pages so I could thank all *the writers and photographers who wrote and photographed me, because these are hard-working and dedicated guys. Only I don't have ten million pages in this book, so I can't even begin to tell you about* all *these fellows. But let me do it this way. Jack Klumpe of the* Cincinnati Post & Times-Star *and Fred Straub of the* Cincinnati Enquirer *each picked what they considered their "best" pictures of me. I'll show them here. They're home-town guys the same as I am. So I guess this will be kind of a home-town book. I wish I had room to show how good all the newspaper photographers are—because I've never met one I didn't like—but that would make this book too big. You'd not be able to lift it. The guys will understand because they're okay. I just want to make sure that the readers understand how much I owe every photographer on every newspaper in every town I've been in. I hope you like these pictures by Jack Klumpe and Fred Straub. I do. There are some real classics here. If I could play baseball just half as good as newspaper photographers take pictures, I'd compile a record that would knock your socks off.*

Fred Straub/*Cincinnati Enquirer*

Fred Straub/*Cincinnati Enquirer*

Rose safe at third as ball gets past LA's Bailey in eighth inning.

Right: Rose out on front end of twin killing in first inning. Braves' second baseman Woodward throws to first to double up Perez who had grounded to shortstop Menke to start play.

Below: Rose safe at second on close play. Houston shortstop Dennis Menke and ump Tom Gorman.

Fred Straub/*Cincinnati Enq*

Fred Straub/*Cincinnati Enq*

Reds' Rose safe at third as SF third baseman waits for ball. Waiting to make the call is ump Al Barlick.

Jack Klumpe/*Cincinnati Post & Times-Star*

Above: Rose slides safely home— right side up for a change—in game with the Cards, June 12, 1969.

Left: Rose cheers for his teammate Tony Perez, who has just hit a homer, as the fans join in the applause in game with the Mets, August 5, 1969.

Top: Rose dives for home plate as the catcher jumps for a high throw St. Louis was the opponent, August 31, 1969.

Bottom: Rose hits the spring training game against the Pirates as man ager Dave Bristol's son, right, in batboy uniform watches. The game was played in Tampa, March 21, 1969.

Jack Klumpe/*Cincinnati Post & Times-Star*

Rose dives for third base and holds onto the bag as Ed Charles misses
the tag in game with New York, May 18, 1969.

Jack Klumpe/*Cincinnati Post & Tim*

Alex Johnson misses the ball, but Rose, on the run, grabs it with his bare hand in game with San Diego, May 4, 1969.

Above: Rose has his feet "taken out from under him" as he is close pitched in game in Tampa with the Tigers, March 19, 1969.

Left: Rose is surprised by a fan who ran onto the field in Met game, August 8, 1969, as Pete was going to his position. It could only happen in a game with the Mets.

Left: Rose scores from third as Dick Dietz (San Francisco) waits for throw from back-up man Jim Davenport (third baseman). Johnson directs traffic.

Below: Reds' manager Dave Bristol restrains Cincinnati star from attacking umpires Ed Vargo and Andy Olsend after Olsend ordered Rose out of game

Fred Straub/*Cincinnati Enquirer*

"Iced tea for 120 guys?" I said the first time. "How do I go about that?"

"Easy, Pete," the other cook said. "Instead of putting in two teaspoons of sugar, dump in two pounds. And lots of luck."

To be fair, I didn't exactly start out as the company cook. I started out over there in Fort Thomas as K. P. If you're a K. P. with that unit you get up at six in the morning and you get to leave when the cooks do, at one in the afternoon. So if I did that kind of schedule, which I kept without complaining, the unit didn't object when I scooted out of the base at one and headed to Cincinnati to play a Saturday or Sunday doubleheader. But then, because that's the way the military does things, they came up with this rule that no guy could be assigned to permanent K. P., which I had been. Kennedy looked at the order and said, "Okay, Pete. From here on out you are going to be a cook's assistant."

That's how I started my new career. The hours were the same. There would be times, playing doubleheaders after feeding 120 guys, that I would be kind of bone weary. But honestly, how could I complain? I had an obligation and I had to fulfill it. No one had forced me into the army. I had joined of my own free will. Actually, these outfits—the reserve units— around this area were real cooperative back then insofar as us jockstraps—military term for athlete, I guess—are called. 'Course what slowed things down was that problem the Green Bay Packers and the National Guard ran into when some senator looked into the matter. He really put the heat on them and he should have. But he pulled the rug out from under the control groups. Control groups are composed of guys who because of their occupation never have to meet too much. It wasn't that way with me. I met every time the unit did; or, if I missed, I made up the missed time with another unit.

The Cincinnati Reds were a big help where my military service requirements were concerned. The guys in the front office knocked themselves out to make everything workable: the military, the requirements of the game, and me.

Always for training our group went back down to Fort Knox, where I had made such a mess of my basic training. I remember there was one weekend encampment down there when I was with the Seymour Avenue unit. I was a driver. This was before I was a cook. Only the truck busted a cylinder. Boy, we were buzzing along that old highway when the dumb thing blew up and so we had to pull over and stop. Well, I did two things real fast. First, I raised the hood of the truck and got our cans of C rations off the manifold where we had been heating them up because we didn't want the mechanics in the service truck to think bad cooking had caused the mess. Then, quick as a rabbit, I jumped in the back of the truck with the other guys, leaving the other driver up front. I wasn't about to stay by the truck until the wrecker arrived. I had to be back in Cincinnati. So we all transferred —and the last I saw of my truck, it was sitting there on the side of the road, not good for nobody but itself any more.

My last commanding officer at Fort Thomas was Gary Bricking, who works for the Cincinnati Gas & Electric Company. He was a straight shooter, giving me no special favors, but made sure all of the guys under him got a square deal. This was when the government had this regulation for athletes. Like if a club has five guys in the army, the guys can go at different times, instead of all at once and emptying a team. Last year I went first from our team, so I went with a different outfit. I spent my time in Fort Knox painting the coal bins white. Then I painted the barracks. But I still ain't no Michelangelo.

But, man, those Saturday and Sunday games used to wear me out, especially when I was cooking for the guys in Fort Thomas. I'd get to the kitchen at six dead tired on Sunday morning because the Saturday schedule—cooking and playing ball—just about exhausted me. That first game on Sunday, to me, was always the worst. I'd been up early Saturday morning, played ball Saturday afternoon, and been up again Sunday morning at 5:30 to start the cycle over again. After the game on Sunday night I would be so pooped I couldn't even stay awake for the "Ed Sullivan Show."

Once when I talked to my barber, Cliff Kuhn, at the Netherland Hilton about how tired I was, all he did was shrug and say, "So that's why you blew that play yesterday. You're the only guy out there with dishpan hands."

Listen, between him and Jan the manicurist it's a wonder I don't get my head cut off instead of my hair. But anyway, the military is behind me now. I'm discharged.

If it helps, I no longer have dishpan hands.

8 Nineteen sixty-four was the year I had a lot of growing up to do. I didn't realize it, though, at the start of the season. I checked into the Congress Inn in Tampa (now they call it King Arthur's) and I got my usual quarters. The motel is only a few blocks from the ball park, which is better, in my estimation, than the way some of the players are situated. Some will be over in Clearwater or St. Petersburg because I guess they got this thing about being on the sandy beaches, but the only thing I ever had was baseball so I never went to the beaches much anyway. Besides, to stay in Clearwater means a long haul to the park. That's where my heart was—at the park and not at the beach. But to each his own, so there I was in the motel, ripe and ready for my sophomore year in the majors.

At least, I told myself, I wasn't the dumb kid I was the other times I had been in Tampa. And I wasn't the dumb kid I had been with the Reds the season before. What I mean is, I hadn't known the score. This is kind of hard to put into words, but I thought I was getting along with the other players real good when I had gone to Tampa the first time. I was on cloud nine back then, just *being* in baseball was all I could think about. But Earl Lawson of the *Cincinnati Post* brought it to my attention how some—not many, just a few—of the white guys on the team resented me a little. I hadn't realized it then. These guys didn't want to go out with me or anything, but on the other hand, there was Frank Robinson and there was Vada Pinson. Those two guys treated me like real brothers.

Once I was even called into the office and this one guy said I had to watch myself because I was hanging around with the colored guys too much and he said a few of the white guys on the team were resenting it.

"Listen," I told him, "these colored guys are the ones who treat me like I'm a human being."

And that's the truth. Frank Robinson knew back then I wasn't the richest kid in the block and he was making lots of money, but he was great to me anyway. He has always been great to me. Even back in high school when I'd show up at the ball park to wear a Reds' uniform and shag flies, Frank Robinson went out of his way to be nice, not only to me, but to all the high school guys.

Frank got along with Curly Smart, the clubhouse guy, who was my dad's uncle. When he found out I was Curly's grandnephew, he was always asking me if I wanted a Coke or some ice cream and stuff like that. He treated me like a human being when I was only a dumb kid. And he did the same when I was a rookie in the majors. Anyway, stuff like some of the guys resenting me isn't important. I proved myself to them and to the club and so the resentment, which was slight at best, is water over the dam. I didn't have time to worry if the guys did or didn't like me. I just wanted to play baseball and do good. But I do remember some lonely moments back then.

Like, one night when we were playing in Chicago

and I had got to the hotel ten minutes after the midnight curfew and my roommate at the time had locked our door and I knocked on it but he wouldn't open it so there I stood in the hall, wondering what to do. Eventually I went upstairs to where Vada Pinson was, he opened the door, and he said, "Come on, Pete. You can sleep in here." Robinson, his regular roommate, was back in Cincinnati, getting his arm worked on. But that's the way the guys were to me. Most of them, as you can see, were swell. The ones who weren't—well, that's water over the dam just like I said.

Anyway, spring training was great and there we were, facing another opening day and ready for another season. We didn't know then that it would be Fred Hutchinson's last year. We didn't know he ran the team that year while most of the time he was in pain. But he never said. That's the kind of man he was. Real class.

I wouldn't exactly call my sophomore year in the major leagues the best I ever had. The old sophomore jinx caught up with me. Listen, for a while there I couldn't do anything right.

The Reds themselves didn't do too bad in 1964. They ended up in second place—St. Louis was first—won 92 and lost 70 games, for a .568 percentage. The Reds scored 660 runs. We had 566 runs scored against us. But Fred Hutchinson got sick and Dick Sisler took over his chores. And as for me, I wasn't the greatest. I just couldn't get going. I ended the season, appearing in only 136 games where the first year I had started in 157 of them. Some of the games I played in I wasn't at second to begin with. I was sitting there, brooding on the bench, and they'd use me as a pinch hitter. As a pinch hitter I went to the plate in 11 games. Out of the 11 trips to the plate as pinch hitter I only got 2 hits. My final batting average was .269, which wasn't good when compared with my first-year average of .273.

That bench duty was no fun. Oh sure, a guy can make money in baseball and be on the bench, but that's not my cup of tea. I mean, you get to be a utility man on a team like the Yankees, you're with a dynasty that is making money. You can make out. But a guy like that makes ten to fifteen thousand a year, has a family, and is expected to live like a big-league player, which usually means having two homes unless you're fortunate enough to be a hometown boy like me. Anyway, I don't dig bench duty and my second year I sure got my share. I can't blame the managers, though. I wasn't hitting. It was nobody's fault but my own.

One day I was sitting there on the bench at Crosley Field, feeling pretty blue, when one of the guys said, "Hey, Pete, will you look at that!" And he pointed out to the bleachers. When I saw what was out there, I wanted to bawl. There was a big sign, hanging up on the bleacher wall.

The sign said, *"ROSE CAN'T BLOOM ON A BENCH!"*

The Lasks had put it there. Joe Lask was the greatest and so is his wife Beatrice and their four kids—Peter, George, Katie, and Jay. They had all got together and made that sign and had put it up there for the world—and my boss—to see. It was a tremendous sign. One of the guys from the front office went out and made them take it down, though, but not before everybody had read it. Joe has been great to me in lots of ways. He's been like a father, helping me with the contracts. He's always giving me advice, and the advice he's always giving me is good. He goes around batting 1.000.

Only there I sat, on the bench. I was sure in some slump. Sometimes when I go into a slump and start striking out I know I'm doing something wrong and I try to figure out what. Like, I could be jerking my head. So I just try to keep my neck in and get all the extra batting practice I can beg, borrow, or steal. Sometimes a guy in a slump will be there because he has come on too strong and he gets too quick. So if that's the case you go out and release some of that tension by swinging forty-five minutes or more. Other times maybe you don't take batting practice because you feel weak so you lay off it for a day. But as far as batting coaches, I listen to only one guy and that's Ted Kluszewski, the big boy from Argo, Illinois, who started with the Cincinnati Reds at first base when I hadn't even started to grade school yet. He's a real slugger. He was with the Reds for eleven years, from 1947 to 1957, then he went to Pittsburgh, and eventually he came back, where everybody loved him. He's got a lifetime batting average of .298. Before he came over to coaching he played in 1,718 games and was at bat 5,929 times, so he knows whereof he speaks when it comes to batting. In 1953 he hit 40 home runs. In 1954 he turned right around and hit 49 more. And in 1955, he hit 47 of them. For five years—between 1952 and 1956—his lowest batting average was .302, and most of the time it was between .316 and .326. Now there is what I call a real pro at the plate. On the other hand, whether I'm in a slump or leading the league, I sure get a lot of free advice from well-meaning people in bars. If I had taken all the advice ever offered me, I wouldn't have lasted in the majors six months.

The point is, you can't listen to three or four guys. Listen to only one guy and believe in him the way I believe in Big Klu.

So there I was in my sophomore batting slump. I did four things to find out what was wrong. I tried using a heavier bat and then I tried using a lighter one. Now I use the same bat most of the time. It's a skinny-handled bat that's thirty-six inches long. The weight, depending on how I feel, will vary between 32½ to 34½ ounces. Like, sometimes in mid-July or August I'll feel strong because hot weather turns me on. Or maybe I've just had a good steak (the night before, that is) and I'll feel extra good. That's when I use the heavier bat. Anyway, I might stand up higher in the box to break the slump. I might move back in the box. Or I might move in closer. But I never change my stance. The first two years in the majors I used the thickest-handled bat there was. It's called a U-1. I choked up that first year and that second year, too. Big Klu said if I used a skinny-handled bat, I'd be able to pull the ball better and he said it was to my advantage to pull the ball because otherwise they'll just play me to hit to left field when I'm batting left-handed. It is a big advantage to hit to all three fields. It took me my first two years in the majors to learn how.

Trouble is, by the time I was running smooth again and worked my way back into the starting lineup we had already lost the pennant by one game. That didn't help my morale much.

I remember when we were playing at Los Angeles I had the uneasy feeling that I might be lifted off the bench and sent back to the minors. Our Triple A team that year was San Diego. I was hitting around 3 for 25 or 3 for 27 or something awful like that and there was talk that the general manager for the San Diego team was coming up to L. A. to take a few players back with him. Now that's the kind of news that can cheer a bench. Since I was the youngest player on the team, I spent a few sleepless nights because I figured this was it. I had even done a dumb thing when I signed my second-year contract for the majors, saying that if I didn't make the big league I would go back to the bushes at the minor-league salary. When I had signed that contract I was sure nothing was going to upset my future. Yeah, I was real cocky back then. But then there were the rumors. And there was the manager from the San Diego team, looking us over.

For some strange reason, they let me stay with the Reds. But I had been scared. I had just learned that there was an awful lot about baseball that I didn't know and that if I was going to last in the majors, I would have to work hard at it.

So I asked if I could play winter ball when the season was over.

They said yes—and there I was, after the regular season, boning up on my Spanish which I didn't know and en route to Venezuela where I had never been. But I was sure looking forward to the warm-weather games. Another winter of doing nothing would have ended my career then and there.

Besides, I was ready for something pleasant. My sophomore year hadn't been the greatest and all that year while I had been sitting on the bench or making a mess of things at bat, I could look over and see something that was breaking all our hearts: we were watching Fred Hutchinson die—inch by inch, game by game. When he had come to spring training that year they said the Bear, which is what they called him because they loved him, was cured. Only all of a sudden he got sick and eventually people were helping him off and on the players' bus. You could tell he was losing weight. The first thing we knew was he couldn't make a road trip with us, and the handwriting was on the wall. The next time I saw Fred Hutchinson, the Bear weighed only 150 pounds. It was as if he had aged—grown old—in two weeks. Seeing him that way destroyed something beautiful in our team. Also, it helped our team, too, because here was a wonderful guy that wants to die in his baseball uniform. The birthday party we had for him was a noisy and beautiful lie because all of us—even him—knew he wasn't going to have any more. Only he never showed what he was feeling. That's the kind of class he had.

The last time I saw Hutch was the last day of the '64 season, before winter ball. Then we went from Venezuela to Santo Domingo to play a weekend series. And we were on the bus from Santo Domingo to downtown and they had this radio on and the announcer said in Spanish that Hutch had died and Reggie Otero started crying right there because Reggie and Hutch were best friends and Reggie couldn't go to the funeral because there he was, in the Dominican Republic.

Damn it all anyway! Hutch always tried to help me grow up. He'd talk to me like a father. He'd tell me not to do certain things and that I could make myself a bigger man by not doing them. And he took the good we had with the bad we had and he'd look only at the good in us. Damn it all anyway! Don't you see? He never saw me have a good year and I owed him that. He's the guy who gave me the chance to be in the major league in the first place. It seems like every year since he died I've hit .300, only he's never seen me do it. He was just the opposite of Dick Sisler, who was also great. I'm sure if Dick could have got another year under his belt he would have done some real good things, too. But he wasn't Hutch. When Dick got mad at you, he'd come and tell you. But if Hutch got mad, he wouldn't tell you. He'd just not talk to you. He'd be silent as the bear they said he was, but you would sure know he wasn't thinking too kindly of you. Dick and Hutch were different, but both had the full respect of all us players. What makes me mad is I like these managers—I've liked every manager I've ever had—only I can't get that real good year in so I can help these guys win the pennant they deserve.

But all of this is neither here nor there. Hutch was dead and there Reggie Otero was sitting beside me on that bus, crying.

I mean, how does a guy say good-bye to a guy?

While I'm on the subject of managers, let me get this in. Let me say this about the front-office guys. I was telling Bob Howsam, our general manager, the other day that it would be great if he would associate more with the players. He liked the idea because he loves baseball as much as any of us, but he said, "Pete, you don't think the players would resent me if I came into the clubhouse more?"

"You *should* come in the clubhouse," I said. "And talk with the guys. Ask the guys if the last road trip was all right, if the plane ride was all right, things like that. Ask them what they feel is right or wrong about things."

"Wouldn't I be interfering with Sparky Anderson's job, though?" Mr. Howsam said.

"No," I said. "What I mean is, you're running a business. It's just like Mr. Ullner out there at Hyde Park Clothes. He goes through the mill and he says, 'Hi, Judy,' and 'How are you doing, Bob?' They all tell him "Hi" and if they do something real good, he comes down to the mill and tells them personally. And if they feel put down, he goes up and asks them what the matter is."

I really feel this way about the front-office guys being in there with us. What could jack up a ball-player better than having the general manager come in when he had just gone 0 for 4 and lost the game on an error and having the general manager say, "Hey, listen, don't let it get you down. We're back in there tomorrow. You'll be all right. You wait and see." That would help a player. Can you imagine Stan Musial, who is a general manager, coming in and saying to the guy, "I've been through a lot of days like you went through, so don't you worry"? Only it's never happened like that with the Reds. Seems like the only time the general manager comes in, there's something wrong. A general manager could find time to come down and talk to us behind the screen. He's the real leader. He is supposed to get inside the players' minds and get to know them and like them for the kind of guys they are. But the only time we see a general manager, we get all uptight and we figure we must have done something awful. It shouldn't be that way. We're all in this game together. The general manager should be allowed some of the fun of it, too.

But I guess that's the way baseball is. And there I was down there playing for the Caracas baseball club in Venezuela. That's the biggest city Venezuela has, twenty-three miles inland from the port of La Guaira. The climate there is generally mild and agreeable, better than Cincinnati winters, with the temperature seldom getting into the nineties or getting below the sixties. It is a town of stone streets, lots of government buildings, and its town square is called the Plaza Bolívar after Simon Bolívar because that's where he was born. All in all, it is a pretty good place to spend the winter because everybody in Venezuela is ape over baseball.

The main reason I was there was to improve, but the money wasn't bad, either. A ballplayer could pick up nearly $1,500 playing a season. Well, I was there with Reggie Otero and he put me through the paces. Soon I was hitting .340, which struck me as an improvement. That year in winter ball down there I think I grew up a little. Having a bad sophomore year in the majors was one of the reasons. The death of Hutch was another.

How did I get along in Caracas? Listen, they loved me down there. I gave them a real show, showing them what hustle was. And I learned Spanish, which was easy because all you have to do is put *el* in front of what you want to say, like, *"El* base on balls, *el* hot dog with *el* mustard, and *el* excuse me" when you want to go to the men's room. I would never win any prizes for my Spanish but I got by and I didn't have anyone running after me shouting, *"El* Yankee, get the *el* out of Caracas." I think one of the reasons they took a shine to me was because I didn't come down there to coast. I came down to learn and to work so I hustled. Some players didn't. They just went for the money. But Reggie worked my tail off. I stayed after practice all the time. I put out as hard as any of the native players. Baseball in that country is a big thing. Maybe that's why they kind of liked me. They saw I loved the game, too.

There would be about a half dozen guys from the States on each of the four teams. I was playing second down there and I'll never forget the first time I played. I made four errors in one inning. I got so mad I just walked right off the field. I was going to go home. You should have heard the stands. They started booing. One guy threw this bottle at me. And I said to myself, "Compared to the Chicago bleachers these guys are rank amateurs." I didn't leave the field. I stayed and played. Why? Because I was growing up a little more, play by play. But I still get a kick out of the way the fans are in Caracas. They gamble. They gamble on every pitch. But they're really enthusiastic. If I make an error, I get booed. When they see me diving for balls, they cheer. There's nothing halfway about them. Besides, I had my work cut out for me. I knew if I didn't improve I might not stay with the majors.

Alex Carrasquel, whose hometown was Caracas and who had been suspended from 1946 to 1949 for playing in the Mexican League, was one of the coaches. He was one of the older guys. He was born in 1912. He used to stay after regular practice and hit me ground ball after ground ball. He hit me ground balls till he was blue in the face, but he was determined to see me get sharp. He is one of the great guys in the business but I've never learned to pronounce his full name, which is Alejandro Aparicio Elroy Carrasquel. He had been a pitcher with the Washington Senators before he got nailed those years for playing in the south-of-the-border league. All I know is, without him and guys like him I'd never have made it. I owe an awful lot to an awful lot of guys.

Helms was down there. Yes, Tommy Van Helms and I roomed together till the wives showed up. He had just finished his rookie year with the Reds and he had a wonderful record. He had only played in two games but had only been at bat in one of them, where he struck out. So he arrived in Caracas with a cheerful smile on his face, a North Carolina drawl, and a .000 average. He had nowhere to go but up which he did, great guy that he is. He played on another team in the league but we both used the same stadium. Some days I'd watch him play. Other days he'd watch me play. There were no away games except one and we were back in Caracas by nightfall. I really enjoyed that league which has nice people who were all nice to me. I remember that our team won the championship. I had led the league in runs scored. Trouble is, there was nothing to do in the evening but watch television, mostly in Spanish, except for the Three Stooges. There were lots of sidewalk cafés there. And Helms and I would shoot pool. We weren't the typical showboating tourists. We tried to be nice people and stay out of trouble. The country was nice to us. We wanted to be nice to it. We were there, except for Christmas at home, from about the middle of October, 1964, to a couple of weeks before spring training started in 1965.

Seemed strange and sad that first day in spring training. I was in my prime. I had been playing ball straight on through and I was anxious to show Hutch how I had improved, but I knew there would be no Fred Hutchinson to show. I got off to a good start in Tampa. I got off to a good start in the season by getting my fair share of hits. On the team that year we had a real powerhouse, which didn't really help us too much because we ended up in fourth place anyway. In 1965 Roberto Clemente led the league with a .329 batting average, Hank Aaron was right behind him with .318, Willie Mays was third with .317, Billy Williams had .315, and I was fifth with .312. That was the year Willie Mays hit 52 home runs. Pinson and I led the league in hits, me with 209 and Pinson with 204. Maloney and Ellis were both hot in 1965. Maloney had a winning percentage of .690 as a pitcher and Ellis had .688. The only guy ahead of them was Sandy Koufax with .765. Tommy Harper scored the most runs that year in our league: 126. Willie Mays scored 118 and I was third, right behind Willie, with 117 runs.

Yeah, 1965 was the year I came of age—a little. I still had a lot to learn. I went to bat 670 times in the season, in which I played in all 162 games. I was hot on doubles. I hit 35 of them, I hit 11 triples, and I surprised myself and everybody else by hitting 11 home runs. They walked me 69 times, but I hustled down to first base anyway. They struck me out 76 times. Listen, no one is perfect. And as I said before, I crossed the plate and scored 117 times. And I tossed a lot of balls into the stands, but nobody—except some front-office bookkeeper—keeps track of those. You know how front-office bookkeepers are. They hate to give away what somebody could be selling.

But tossing balls into the stands is something I've been doing a long time. I've been called to the front office for throwing balls into the stand. They said they were going to take the price of the balls out of my check and then they look at me like my high-school teachers used to do back in Western Hills High School and try to get me to see the error of my ways. The next game I toss more balls into the stands. Call me a slow learner. But the way I feel is, that if a ball gets hit into the stands and bounces back out onto the field because the stands were empty and nobody was there to catch it I'm going to throw the ball *back* into the stands because it isn't my fault the stands aren't packed, is it? They can take the price of the balls out of my pay. I'll still keep throwing balls back into the stands. Other players do the same thing, but not as often as I do. I do it on the road as well as at home.

You'd be surprised how many people want a game

ball. This is the only game I know where a guy will pay a hundred bucks for a seat in the hopes he'll get his hands on a three-dollar baseball. They simply have *got* to have that baseball. I agree with the front office that if I throw the ball back in the stands—hard —somebody might get hurt and I think that is what worries them, but I never try to push it hard unless I know personally the guy that is catching it. Chances are, I'll go over and *hand* the guy the ball. I throw a couple of balls back into the stand each game, which means each year I'll toss out around four hundred balls.

I remember one time in 1969 I was so happy we had won this game that I threw the ball up in there because it was the last out and we had won. Well, when I got to the clubhouse Wayne Granger said he wanted the ball because it was a record-setting thing, his ninetieth appearance in a baseball game, the all-time National League record, and that made me feel sad because I had tossed the ball away. You'd be surprised the different reason us baseball players collect baseballs. I must have at least two dozen. I got the ball I hit my thousandth hit with. I got the ball I hit my two hundredth hit with. I got the ball that I set the record for triples in the minors with. I've got an autographed ball from Stan Musial and another one from Ted Williams.

By the time the 1966 season got under way, I was—reasonably—matured. That was the year they brought in Dave Bristol to run the team. We didn't do too well, finishing in seventh place, beating out only Houston, Chicago, and New York. That was the year Tommy Harper was hot on stolen bases, stealing twenty-nine of them, but Lou Brock led the league in thievery because he stole seventy-four during the season. Maloney was a hot pitcher, his percentage being .667. McCool had eighteen saves. And Maloney trailed only Sandy Koufax when it came to the most strike-outs per nine innings. Koufax's average was 8.83 and Maloney's was 8.65. We all played our hearts out because we wanted to make Dave Bristol look good, but it just wasn't in the cards. When the 1966 season ended, we had won 76 games and lost 84, and there we were, feeling blue, 18 games out of first place. That wasn't as bad as Chicago, which was 36 games behind the first-place Los Angeles team, but it wasn't good.

There were a few things, though, that cheered me personally. For the second straight year I had finished in the .300s. In 1965 my average had been .312: in 1966 it was .313. That was the year they switched me to third, which wasn't the greatest place to put me, but when they said go, I didn't fuss, I went. Of the 156 games I played that year, 16 of them were at third. The rest I played at second. I never pretended to be the best third baseman in the world and I think, even though I tried, I proved my point that I wasn't. Out of 654 times at bat in 1966 I had 205 hits, including 16 home runs which, to that point, was the most I had ever hit in a major-league season. But I hit fewer triples—only 5 of them. I was hot on doubles; I hit 38 of them. I ended the 1966 season scoring 97 runs and in the runs-batted-in column the scorers put a 70. I walked 37 times. I struck out 61 times. I stole only 4 bases because, as I said earlier, I'm not exactly the greatest base stealer they got in the majors.

So the season was over and we sat around watching the Baltimore American League team take the World Series from Los Angeles in four straight games. It seemed strange sitting there watching Frank Robinson in the very first game hit a homer for Baltimore.

I missed that guy but that's the way baseball is. And when that fourth-inning homer of his in the fourth game nailed down the series I felt kind of sad. That could have been us in there.

But that's okay. Since 1901 in the National League the Reds have only finished first four times. Between 1876 to 1900 the Reds had only finished first once—and that was in the American Association in 1882. But as we all said when we left the clubhouse that last time after the 1966 season, "Well, listen, there's always next year!" You'd think with finishing first only five times in the hundred years the Reds have been playing baseball that pretty soon we've got to have a hot year.

But before the next season—1967—started, I had another kind of growing up to do.

9 A year after Pepper Martin and Paul Waner died, I went to Vietnam. Why? Well, I had never met Joe DiMaggio and there I was, standing around Shea Stadium in New York and this one guy came up and said, "How would you like to go to Vietnam when the season is over?" I said, "I'm not sure because I don't know what my plans are yet." He said, "Well, Joe DiMaggio is going. And I'll tell you who else is going. There is . . ." But he didn't have to say any more. I cut in and said, "Count me in." A guy will do anything to meet his baseball hero, won't he? Joe DiMaggio had always been mine. Now there is a real good player. Whenever I think of a guy having class, I think of Joe DiMaggio. He had class that wouldn't quit. Babe Ruth might have been the first home-run champion that the American League ever had, winning himself the title two years in a row (1920 and 1921), then coming back and winning it two more years in a row (1923 and 1924), and then coming back and winning it six years in a row (from 1926 to 1931), but still Joe DiMaggio was my idol. He was home-run champion first in 1937, the year we had that big flood here in the Ohio Valley. Then he was home-run champion eleven years later, in 1948, the year the incline stopped running in Cincinnati. In 1941 he had

the most runs batted in in the American League, 125.
In 1948, he had the most again, with 155. He was the
American League batting champion in 1939 (.381) and
in 1940 (.352). In 1939 and in 1941 he was voted the
American League's Most Valuable Player. Incidentally, in 1939 when they named Joe that, a guy from
the Reds got the most valuable player title in the National League. That was Bucky Walters. Anyway,
there sits Joe DiMaggio in the Baseball Hall of Fame
with his career average of .325, having played from
1936 to 1951, and there we were meeting in his restaurant in San Francisco, down there on the Fisherman's
Wharf, and I was gawking at him like a tongue-tied
kid. I mean, actually, the first time I met him all I
could do was stand there, my mouth open, and think
I was about the luckiest guy in the world, getting to
meet Joe. Here was the guy who put the others to
shame—in *my* estimation, that is.

When I had been running around in the Knot Hole
league, this guy had been in the majors. Meeting Di-
Maggio was, for me, like meeting everybody rolled
into one: Rogers Hornsby, Chuck Klein, Mel Ott,
Ducky Medwick, Ralph Kiner, Lou Gehrig, Jimmy
Foxx, Hank Greenberg, Stan Musial, Ty Cobb, Tris
Speaker, and—even—Ernie Lombardi. No wonder I
was speechless in Joe's restaurant. I had every reason
to be.

And there we were, in this plane we had caught at
Traverse Air Force Base on our way to Vietnam by
way of Anchorage, Alaska, and Tokyo. It was called
the World Air Lines, which doesn't mean too much to
me because what it was, was a plane that had nothing
but military personnel on it. There were no first-class
seats. And the crowd of guys on the plane weren't
singing or anything like that. The minute the plane

lifted off from the air force base, most of them fell silent because they didn't have the United States underneath them any more. Some were going to Japan for duty but most were going to Vietnam. They had little reason to be cheerful. The sight again of a landing field in the United States would be—for them—a long time coming. Or maybe never. I could sense this in them. It tore me up, knowing how they felt. A guy can grow up fast in the company of fellows like that.

There was one good thing, though. No generals were on the plane and since we ballplayers were traveling as GS-15s, we were (temporarily) treated like lieutenant colonels, which wasn't bad for a guy who drove a truck in the reserves or was the company cook. I guess I'm about the only company cook in the military that was treated like a lieutenant colonel. On the other hand the *good* company cooks didn't need to be treated like officers. Everybody, including the officers, treated them like royalty.

We got a good tail wind so the plane didn't put down at Anchorage. But even so, we didn't have enough gas to reach all the way to Tokyo, so we landed at a Japanese airport outside the big city itself. We got gassed up and took right off again. About seventeen hours later there we were, getting ready to shoot a landing in Saigon. I was sure glad to see Vietnam because seventeen hours in that little seat hadn't been too comfortable. There wasn't much walking-around room on the plane. The landing at Saigon kind of took me by surprise and made me feel, for real, that there was sure a war going on.

One minute we were hanging up there in the sky. Then next minute—swoop!—we were in a power dive, aimed straight at the runway below. Only at the last possible moment did the pilot level off that baby. Otherwise we would have been a permanent part of the landscape. The other passengers took this kind of landing in stride. It didn't shake them as much as it shook me. But it really shook me. The pilot had announced on the intercom why he was landing that way.

". . . To keep the enemy from shooting at us if we made a long and easy approach, the kind we would have made in the States," he said.

Then, zoom! Down we went!

We climbed out of the plane. I was sure glad to stretch my legs. Then we went through customs, where they asked me if I had anything to declare, and I said, "I declare that was the wildest landing I have ever made." They just gave me a look—I think Augie Donatello had given them staring lessons—and let me pass. The other ballplayers and me rode into Saigon and I've got news for you. Saigon is sure a lot different from anything I had ever seen. That place is amazing.

"Listen, Joe," I said, as we rode to the hotel, "look out there. I just can't believe the poverty."

I meant it. Compared to Saigon, the poorer sections of Cincinnati is where the rich people live. Also, everybody and his brother had a bicycle or a motorbike. Somebody told me once over there that the government had worked out a deal where if a guy put up so much money, he got a motorbike. I don't know whether this is true or not because I'm no political science kind of guy, but I do know everybody had wheels. That, plus the poverty, was the first thing that impressed me about Saigon. Only something else was there, too.

"Pete," Joe said, pointing out his side of the car window, "There's the war for you."

I looked. I saw a bombed-out building. As we drove to the hotel, buildings like that became ordinary sights. We passed the United States Embassy, where there had been a lot of bombing. Yes, they really had themselves a war going on over there.

The interesting thing about the traffic in Saigon was that if some local guy didn't run you down with a motorbike maybe some nut driving an army jeep would. At least, that's the way it seemed at first. Only nobody hit nobody. I still can't see why not. The streets were filled with so many military vehicles—jeeps, trucks—that the town had the appearance of an army camp. Anyway, dead tired from the long plane ride, we reached the hotel and tried to hit the sack. Only before we could get undressed, we were sitting around the room, shooting the bull, and in walked Martha Raye. She was wearing her colonel's uniform. Well, she and Joe DiMaggio got to talking because since he had been connected with Marilyn Monroe, he and Martha sure had a lot of Hollywood friends in common. To hear them talk was to be in the company of all the golden people Hollywood had. I just sat and listened. How could I explain to them the wonders of Anderson Ferry? They had seen everything and met everybody. Anderson Ferry wouldn't have stood a Chinaman's chance.

After a while, Martha Raye got to talking to me, too, which was awful nice of her. There's real class. I can still remember her, sitting there in that hotel room, and saying how we were great guys to come over and see the fellows and how we should be.

"Just talk to the boys about back home," she said. "Just be yourself and the guys will really appreciate it. . . ."

See, we were a different type show than the kind

Bob Hope puts on because, to tell the truth, we weren't a show at all. We were not there to play baseball. We were there just to walk around and talk to the guys and—maybe—for one brief moment get their minds off all the stuff that was making them sad and lonely. What we were on was a handshaking kind of tour. I figured they would be pleased as punch to see Joe DiMaggio. I wondered a lot of the times what *I* was doing there, though. Joe was famous. I was a nobody.

All the time we were sitting around the hotel room that first night I kept hearing things like boom, boom, boom, which they explained to me were mortars being lobbed into the city. And all night long, there were constant shooting noises which they said was to keep the enemy down. That first night I got the idea for real, that everybody was playing for keeps. It is one thing to sit in a hotel, waiting for the bus to take you to the game, and read about how this or that building got blown to smithereens. But it's another to be sitting in a hotel room, making chitchat, in the town where your building might be next. In Vietnam there are no front lines. The front line could be down there on the delta or could be in the hotel lobby. A guy couldn't relax anywhere. He had to learn to live with it, though, or he'd go ape. I got the same feeling in the hotel that night that I get when I turn my back to the bleacher bums at Wrigley Field. Any minute you expect the sky to fall down. Maybe they should do the bleachers in Chicago the way they do the grandstands down there in Venezuela. The ushers are cops. And they're all equipped with submachine guns to keep the spectators under control. But that's another matter. What I'm talking about here is Vietnam.

Well, for our first couple of days there, they took us down to the Mekong Delta, where we visited the advisory teams, which is what they called the guys. There would be four or five of these American guys out in the middle of the boondocks, out there in nowhere, telling the Vietnamese how to fight and stuff like that. The place sure wasn't Cincinnati. The Mekong River is called the River of the Nine Dragons. The delta is a sticky place of muddy beaches and mangrove swamps. Cambodia is a whoop and a holler over thataway. Mud is everywhere and the mud, they say, is just about the stickiest they got in the world. The swamps are filled with snakes. The navy had a bunch of pennywhistle gunboats painted green. These gunboats would zoom along the river and play along the canals, trying to keep the waterway open for regular traffic. The enemy had rockets hidden in the jungle. Sometimes a gunboat would get nailed. Around there, I saw my first water buffalo. And there were, here and there, rice fields. There were all kinds of trees: coconut, litchis, papayas, mangoes, and things like that. Everything grows there real good, thanks—they say— to the monsoons which fertilize the rice crop. Helicopters are always up there, bringing stuff in and out, or—as airborne gunboats—shooting enemy sampans that try to sneak by in the gloom of the night. Sometimes things get so scary and so noisy that the *son ca,* which the delta farmers calls the skylark, will stop his singing altogether. To stroll in a rice field alone is impossible. A district chief, one of the natives, said no. Why? He couldn't spare the thirty men needed to protect me if I went. Could I sit in the café in the corner of town, near the canal? No. There were snipers across the canal. The snipers wouldn't shoot much at natives but a foreigner was always a target. So you can't exactly call our junket a milk run.

Even the helicopter ride from Saigon down to the

delta wasn't a milk run. We followed this Route 4, which was the main—and about the only—road connecting the two places. The officer in the plane with us had warned us about the trip.

"I'm going to show you," he said, "the biggest traffic jam you've ever seen in your whole life."

I was impressed and I guess Joe DiMaggio was, too.

So off the bird went, clattering through the sky. Listen, we had only risen around twenty-five feet when the pilot leveled the chopper off—and away we went, at treetop level, 110 knots an hour. We'd look out, see a tree coming straight at us, and just at the last minute we'd barely skim over its highest branches.

"Ground fire," he said through the intercom. "That's the reason we're flying low. They won't have time to get a bead on us."

"Swell," I thought and held my breath as he skimmed another tree. Compared to that ride, the Wildcat at Coney Island is a kiddy car.

Sometimes we'd get as high as fifty feet off the ground. Other times we'd clatter along just twenty feet up there.

"I'm looking for Charlie," the pilot said, meaning the enemy, "and Charlie is looking for me."

Below us, almost where we could reach out and touch but not quite, was the road—jammed with all kinds of traffic, military and civilian. The traffic wasn't moving. It was *all* stalled. On either side of the road were the wet rice paddies. Then, nothing.

"Charlie knocked out a bridge last night," the pilot said. "That's what slowed everything down. Too far to go back to town," he added. "So they're waiting."

Moments later we landed in a village, shook hands, and said good-bye to the pilot. But listen, I'll never forget that ride. Then we got on boats and went down the river to where these soldiers were, stuck in the middle of nowhere. We'd go into a place and Joe Di-Maggio would walk up to them, say, "Hi, I'm Joe Di-Maggio," and you should have seen the pleased looks on the faces on the guys. Joe would say, "I'm Joe Di-Maggio, an old broken-down ballplayer, and this here is Pete Rose, one of the modern-day ballplayers, and this here is Bob Fishel, of the New York Yankees." Bob was their public relations director. Well, we'd sit and talk to them for about fifteen minutes. All of them were such nice guys. I mean that. Like this one place we visited, they had built showers for the natives. And there would only be five or six of them, living there in that outpost. Mostly we talked about baseball, but they were willing to talk about anything because other than the mailman coming by, they wouldn't have seen another American for months. The guys might have been appreciative, and they all were, but they could never appreciate what Joe and I were doing as much as Joe and I appreciated them. Yeah, down there on the delta was really something that would inspire a guy and all the while it would be tearing his heart out. Those guys were the greatest.

One of them said that the night before we had showed up, they had had a little action.

"The enemy show up?" I said.

"That," said one of them, "and we shot a tiger on the prowl."

"There are tigers here, too?" I said.

"There's everything here," they said, "and most of it will kill us some day."

That kind of talk, delivered ordinary like talking about the weather, hits a guy where he lives.

Another time, down there, one of the generals came up and said to Joe and me that he wanted to take us on what he called a milk run so we got in the chopper with him and took off at treetop level, headed to just this side of the Cambodian border. Well, we landed at the edge of this one little village and there, stretched out dead on the street in front of us, were six North Vietnamese regular soldiers. They were there in the afternoon sun, covered only by bamboo. I actually touched one of them with my foot and listen, I'll never do *that* again. I asked why they were covered with bamboo.

"Their people will come back and get the bodies," the general said. "They like to retrieve their own dead and to bury them."

We walked through the dirty little village to a school building which had been bombed but was still being used. When we walked around behind the school I saw the most amazing thing I had ever seen in my life. The school had let out. There were about 250 grade-school kids all standing there in the school yard, boys and girls together, mixed up. Then, somebody—I guess it was a teacher—blew a whistle. Well, the kids standing on the school-yard cement all took two steps forward and the ones that had to go to the bathroom stopped and went right there! That's one picture I don't think they'll ever show you in a doctor's office when you're reading *National Geographic*. But that sure was something. Sad, too. I'm not telling about it here to make fun. Don't ever get that idea.

Then there was another little village, hardly bigger than a smelly bus stop, and we stayed there that night, ate chow with the guys, went to a movie with them, and everything. Most of the soldiers there had *mamasans* who are girls—real little ones—and they shine the soldier's shoes and keep his clothes laundered. I'll never forget that little village. Vietnam has hundreds like it but to me this one will always be special. A few months after Joe DiMaggio and I had visited there, spent the night, and talked with the guys, I read that the little village had been blown off the face of the earth. Everybody in it had been killed. I could only think of the faces of the soldiers I had seen there, the way they laughed at the open-air movie, the way the little kids were, sitting there, shining shoes, and all of it got mixed up together in my mind—and for a while I was too shook to speak. They had been there. Now they were all gone. I felt as if I had lost a hundred friends in an awful accident. And I had.

Somewhere down on the delta was this place that had about fifteen or twenty gunboats, but there were no barracks. The guys ate, slept, and lived on the boats. I remember when we walked up to the dock the guys were sitting around, eating C rations, talking back and forth from one boat to the other. We could look out into the river and way over there, in the distance, we could see other gun boats raking the shoreline with fire from machine guns and rockets— and here these guys sat, eating C rations out of a can, and expressing gratitude that Joe DiMaggio had thought enough to drop around and actually see them.

"Hey," one of them said, "we're not that important. You ought to be back there in Saigon where the generals are."

"This is where we belong," Joe said—and he spoke for all of us.

And so we shook hands with those wonderful guys and over there, at the edge of the dock, was a bunch of South Vietnamese soldiers and with them was just about the youngest general I had ever seen. But I could tell, by the way they were jabbering at each other, that these guys really respected their Vietnamese general even though he did look like a kid still wet behind the ears. We talked to the U.S. commander there who told us that those fellows loved that general because he liked to get out and rub elbows with his men and that if ever there was any fighting, he'd be right in the thick of it. It gave me a real good feeling, seeing him, standing with his men, joking with them, patting them on the back, like he is fighting for what they're fighting for. Whenever I hear talk back home about how dumb and hopeless these South Vietnamese soldiers are, I don't say a word, but the picture of that young general comes to mind and I hope someday he will be able to lead his guys to peace. But I don't know now if he's alive or dead.

As for the Vietnamese getting excited because Joe DiMaggio was visiting, well, as soldiers say, it never happened, which I am sorry to report here. I don't think the South Vietnamese are too baseball-minded. Maybe they're too busy fighting and dying. But they could tell by the way our guys raved over Joe that Joe was somebody special. So they treated him accordingly. I'm glad of that because Joe DiMaggio will always be "somebody special."

Then we went back to Saigon, where bombs went off all night and the next mortar might be the one with your name on it. We'd go up on the roof of the hotel each night and watch the deadly fireworks. It was a scary sight. Then, we'd talk over where we'd been that day and feel sad and good all over again because where we had been had been visiting the hospital wounded. These were the evacuation hospitals that received guys, via helicopter, straight from the battle scene that had caused them pain. We must have visited hundreds of guys but a few I'll never forget. I hated these hospital tours not because I didn't like the guys but because that's the way I am. I would rather have gone on a reconnaissance with the guys and maybe got killed than visit hospitals, but I went because I had to; I owed these guys more than I could ever repay. But, oh, the sights we saw. . . .

Like, we saw this one kid they had to strap down. He had gone crazy. He had actually gone crazy. He had fallen off the back of a truck, had landed on the back of his head, and that was all she wrote. Seeing him, struggling to be free, made me want to cry. It actually did. The guy should have been home, playing baseball or maybe seeing his girl, or things like that which, for him, would never again take place at all. Hospitals tear me up.

Like, I went and visited this one Negro. Now he was a real good-looking guy from somewhere in Pennsylvania. He was sitting up in his bed, talking normal, and he seemed okay. We talked about Pennsylvania for a while, then about football. Only I couldn't figure out why he was in the hospital. They had told us that when we talk to the guys not to be afraid to talk about their injuries, so I figured I might as well go ahead.

"Well," I said, "are you about ready to go home? What did happen to you anyway?"

He pulled the sheet back and showed me.

"That damned North Vietnamese soldier threw a grenade at me," he said like he was talking about the weather. "And when he did it, he blew off my legs."

There he sat, nineteen years old, and he was saying, still in the same matter-of-fact way, "I wish I could go back out there tomorrow and find the guy who did it. . . ."

Can you see why hospitals tear me up?

Now and then, there would be kind of happy endings. Like, when Joe and I talked to this one kid he is standing there, bent over, looking at the floor, and when he turned, man, I saw the biggest gash I had ever seen in a guy's head. The doctor said he had taken a piece of metal big as my fist out of the back of this guy's neck.

"Oh God," I thought, "This poor guy is standing around here, waiting to die."

But the doctor said no. "This kid," he told us, "is going to be fine because his spinal column wasn't hurt." And he said the kid was happy because they had told him he could be back out there in a couple of weeks, fighting again.

I think, going through those hospitals, I saw every kind of injury ever thought up. Nine out of ten, though, were missing arms and legs and fingers. Blown off.

We went to this one ward where the nurse said, "Do you want to see our Charlies?" In Vietnam "Charlies" were the V. C.'s. So Joe and I went in to see their Charlies. I'll say one thing: the Charlies were treated just as good as our own guys were treated. Their wards were air-conditioned the same as the wards our guys were in. Being hurt makes brothers of all men—and the girls. Like, this one girl was in bed and we asked what happened to her. The nurse said the girl was a North Vietnamese squad leader that the South Vietnamese had caught. The nurse said they hooked her up to a generator and had tried to electrocute her, but the only thing they had done was paralyze her. So there she was in the hospital bed. She couldn't move. She just lay there, looking straight up at the ceiling. The nurse said she would eventually be all right. If she had been in Cincinnati, she still would have been riding the school bus to high school every day, listening to records, giggling with other girls, and maybe having some dumb ballplayer fall in love with her. But she wasn't in Cincinnati.

These soldiers in the hospital told me lots of things. They said that the rice-paddy workers would be out there, wading around the water, working the rice paddies, nice as pie. Only after the soldiers walked by, the workers would reach down, pick up a gun, and start shooting at them. I mean, what they were saying was a guy couldn't tell which was the enemy and which was the friend.

Ward after ward after ward—filled with people the war had got to.

"I can't take much more of this," I told Joe.

He nodded because he had class and he understood. Only we didn't leave. We stayed. . . .

Other times we went other places to see the guys. One place was where an advisory team, living in foxholes, was playing nursemaid to big fifteen-inch guns. While we were standing around saying hello, one of the big guns went off, again and again, right behind us. Boy, did that scare me! This gun was shooting and clearing the way for a squad that had attacked some North Vietnamese up ahead. After the gun fired each time you could look out there and see the smoke where it had hit. I was scared, sure, but even as I write this I'm more scared. My brother is over there right now, somewhere in the forest along the Cambodian border. Only he can't look, say hello, and leave. He has to stay there.

Once Joe and I went up in a chopper to look at the

central highlands and to visit some of the guys stationed there. All we could see from the air was a land marked with bomb craters, like bombs had clobbered every inch of the terrain. The place was about the loneliest place I had ever seen, like we were up there, clattering along in our chopper, and looking down on another world that people hadn't got around to building cities or farms in yet.

On the other hand, we got away from some of that sadness when we went to visit the aircraft carrier *Intrepid*. We flew like gooney birds, strapped in backwards, so the sudden stop on the carrier deck wouldn't snap our heads off. We stayed on the *Intrepid* a couple of days and listen, we had some real good quarters. The navy sure does things up brown, doesn't it? All around the ship they had these little television sets and each night Joe and I did a closed-circuit television show, with the guys all over phoning in and asking us questions. But the work of the *Intrepid* went right on. Each morning at about six the jets were hurled off on missions. Meanwhile, we waited there, sloshing around in Tonkin Bay, waiting for them to return and hoping they would.

I'll never forget the one day that all 3,500 guys on that ship let out a great big roar. The news had come in that one of their fellows who had been shot down had been rescued. I'll never forget that roar if I live to be a million. I've heard many crowds roar, but never like that. It was, in some ways, the most beautiful roar ever made.

Joe and I liked to watch the planes land and take off that carrier because that's the craziest arrival and departure any traveler could have. Once I stood there, right underneath where the planes took off. In the morning, it happened. Around six. They sure go to work early in the navy. And zoom, there they went right over me, seems like only inches away, but I guess it was more. The planes don't really fly off. They are catapulted off. Wild ride. Talk about laying down a patch of rubber at an intersection.

Landing is even more Mickey Mouse. They got these four cables stretched across the flight deck. Up there, in the sky, the planes are circling. Then, in they come, one right after the other, thirty seconds apart. As soon as one plane touches down, it snags one of these cables, and snap! the plane is stopped. But breathing down its tail is another one, shooting its landing. They got no time to relax and say, "Whew." The second one plane touches down, one guy catches the cable that hooked the plane, another guy runs out, unhooks it, and before you know what is happening, they got this plane on an elevator that's lowering it— fast—down to the hangar deck. Meanwhile another plane has landed and is getting untangled from the cable fast because another plane is up there, right behind it, zeroed in on the runway, and coming fast. Those guys sure work hard. And they're a great team. Now and then a plane will miss the cable. It might bounce on the deck and there's no waiting around. It powers up and takes off again, to go back up there in the sky and join its buddies circling, waiting to land. If at first you don't succeed, as my old teachers used to say, try and try again.

One morning just before one of the planes took off, Joe got a big piece of chalk and wrote things about Ho Chi Minh on one of the bombs they were putting on the planes. One of the things he wrote was, "Down With Ho!" When the pilot came back he told Joe that the bomb he wrote "Down With Ho!" on had wiped out a bridge. I never wrote anything on any of the bombs.

I don't know why. Maybe it's because I've always been a poor speller.

But that *Intrepid* was sure some boat. It had 3,500 guys on it. Its landing deck is as big as a football field and they say the *Enterprise* is twice as big. Every morning we'd get up and watch the guys take off. They'd be gone two hours, and then they would come back for what they called "recovery." There would be a meeting, lunch, and after lunch another bunch of guys would fly away. I liked staying on that thing. It was a real experience. But I don't think I'd care to be the guy who had to fly one of those planes off and on that postage stamp out there in the ocean. I'd rather face a dozen Gaylord Perrys.

After that, we went back to Saigon and visited more hospitals and got sad all over again. I'm not a hospital-visiting kind of guy. Being an athlete, I suppose, made me even more aware of what had happened to these brave fellows. I just couldn't take it, day after day, visiting guys who had their arms and legs blown off, or seeing a nice young guy sitting there and going crazy, or be there when a guy would start bawling. Listen, I went to this one ward where this one soldier was. He was actually holding a baby in his arms. The little thing weighed only three pounds, only there it was, eight months old. They said he had found this baby in the rice paddies where somebody had left it to die, and when he got injured, he refused to give up the kid. He told them he was going to bring the baby back to the States with him. He had a real bad leg injury. He was in bed, holding this baby, the cutest little baby you ever saw, and after that I went back outside fast because I felt like I was about ready to bust out bawling myself.

But Joe DiMaggio was, as I say, the greatest every

minute of every day over there. I learned a lot from him. He made all the fellows feel right at home. He had so much class I could hardly believe it. And, as I said before somewhere else in this book, he gave me a shower and I gave him one. It was one of those places where it was so hot the two of us couldn't sleep so we decided to heck with it, and we got up to take a shower that would cool us off. It was an outdoor shower like they have in the field, the kind where you pour a bucket of water in the thing and the water runs through on the guy taking the shower. I did it for Joe and he did it for me. There I was, standing up on this chair, pouring a bucket of water through this big thing for Joe's shower and I could hear, close by, bombs and mortars going off. It was sure scary. But we did get cooled off and now I have something to tell my grandchildren: I'm probably the only guy in baseball who ever gave Joe DiMaggio a shower.

We used to shoot the bull about baseball and everything. Call me a Joe DiMaggio fan because that's exactly what I am. It was a great honor for me to be in the company of this fellow. He was just the opposite of what people had told me about him. They had said he was quiet and never said much, but with me he was talkative, heartwarming, and kind. I can still remember some of the bull sessions, me wearing fatigues and a jungle hat the First Cavalry had given me and old Joltin' Joe, the Yankee Clipper, was wearing fatigues and that green baseball cap from the Oakland Athletics. Yeah, those were great moments for me. He was in his fifties and there I was, the kid from Sedamsville, hardly dry behind the ears. He had thirteen years in the big leagues, wrapping it all up in 1951, and while he had been doing that, I had been down there in Bold Face Park, playing my heart out for the Knot Hole League. There he sat with 1,736 games under his belt. He had been to bat 6,821 times in the majors and had struck out only 369 of those times. He had 1,390 runs to his credit, with a lifetime batting average of .325 and a slugging average of .579. There I was, sitting with the guy who had played in ten different World Series—from 1936 to 1951—and had batted 51 times in them, had made 8 runs in them, and as he sat across from me at night, chewing the fat, was also a member of the Baseball Hall of Fame because in 1955 that's where they put him. We talked about baseball and we talked about our homes. He was from Martinez, California, only there we were, a million miles away from nowhere, hearing bombs go off and hearing mortars go off. Yet I would not trade those evening bull sessions with Joe DiMaggio for all the gold in the world. There are some things money can't buy—and being with Joe DiMaggio is one of them. There he stood, six foot two, and there I stood, five feet eleven. But height means nothing where class is concerned. He has class I'll never have—and that's a fact.

Sometimes Joe and I would go about in real style, like the times we visited General Westmoreland's headquarters. One time the general gave us an autographed picture of himself. You ought to see the headquarters these guys have. It's like a miniature Pentagon. It's got wall-to-wall carpeting, air conditioning, and the works. And most of the times that the generals ride in cars, they ride in air-conditioned ones with the windows shut tight. The reason they can't travel around with the windows down is that somebody might come along and lob in a hand grenade. The stories we used to hear! Listen, they say some of these North Vietnamese pay kids to throw bombs and grenades. That scares me. One minute you'll see some Vietnamese go by on a bike—one I saw had a family of five!—and the next minute there will be some poor little kid, waiting to toss a bomb. That's no way to do kids. They have a hard enough time growing up over there as it is.

Another time Joe and I went riding with those guys patrolling the delta, and it didn't help the war too much but they let me run the gunboat for a short distance. We were going up the river to this one village and they told me to keep the boat in midstream because on both sides of the river, hiding in the green, were North Vietnamese. That's one time I didn't kid around. I stayed right out there in the middle, wishing the river was a lot wider than it was. When we reached the village, they let me fire a mortar. There were these soldiers, dug real deep in foxholes, and they said, "Go ahead, Pete, try a round." I did. But I don't think I helped the war much. I had my eyes shut and my hands over my ears. And there was Joe Di-Maggio, laughing at me.

Of course I could go on forever about that trip to Vietnam but I don't know. Even now as I put it down here on paper all the smells and noises and feelings —real *deep* feelings—come back and I get the lonely feeling all over again. After seventeen days we left the war zone which, to me, was all of South Vietnam. Joe and I talked about it, figuring we must have shaken a million hands, all of them belonging to brave men. We flew back by way of Manila, Guam, Hawaii, and San Francisco.

When the plane took off from Saigon, all the soldiers in the plane gave out a big yell. It was like a noisy sigh of relief because there they were, up there in the sky, and down there—going away fast—was

Saigon with all its bikes and all its hurts and its little kids, some who shined shoes for the soldiers, and some who held grenades and waited, in alleys, for the right target to come along. When we landed in San Francisco, Joe DiMaggio took me to a different airport so I could get my plane home. I wanted to get home and so did he.

I wanted to remember—and I wanted to forget.

10 In 1967 I began to get rolling. Dave Bristol and his wad of tobacco were still running the show. I ended the season still in the .300 column, but just barely. I inched in with a batting average of .301, which pleased just about everybody but me. Clemente had .357 that year in the National League and guys like Gonzalez, Alou, Flood, and Staub were ahead of me, too. Pinson was stealing bases like crazy the 1967 season, 26 of them. He also led the league in triples, belting out 13 of them. That was the year of young Gary Nolan with his 2.58 earned run average, slightly ahead of the guy who drives me crazy, Gaylord Perry, who had an average of 2.61. Ted Abernathy was credited with 28 saves, leading the league in that column. He also pitched in the most games that year, 70 in all. He tied with Perranoski for that exhausting honor.

That was the year I moved to the outfield, playing in 123 games out there. I also played 35 games at second base, which meant I played all told in 158 games in 1967, going to bat 585 times, to accumulate 176 hits of which 32 were doubles, eight were triples, and 12 were home runs. I scored 86 runs in 1967, drew 56 walks, and fanned 66 times. But the Reds finished 14½ games out of first place, winning 87 games and losing 75. St. Louis beat Boston in the World Series, four games to three. And what 1967 was, was over.

But numbers by themselves don't tell the story of the guys and the stuff we got into and—sometimes—out of. Before this book is over I got to tell you about umpires and traveling and things like that and this chapter seems as good as any. But let's go through 1968 first and see how the season fared because that was the year I broke my thumb, which is not exactly earthshaking but it did keep me on the bench for a while, a place I'd rather not be. I'd never make a good baseball fan. My kick is *playing* the game, not *watching* the game played.

Anyway there I was with that broken thumb and there I was on the outside looking in for twenty-one straight days. I was getting pretty fed up with being a fan when we arrived for a stand in Pittsburgh. It was raining one day so there was no real workout. We couldn't do practice hitting because of the canvas on the field, and I guess Dave Bristol felt sorry for me so he said, "Come on, Pete."

We went out there to left field by the scoreboard and he had this regular rubber ball with him and a skinny kind of bat and I was trying to strike him out against the wall. We were playing like kids do, really, because that is also the way baseball players are. Anyway, after I'd tossed him a bunch, he said, "Here, Pete, you take the bat and let me try it." So he took the red rubber ball and I took the bat, batting left-handed, and I was surprised because I thought my thumb would be hurting only it wasn't. That was on Wednesday. We were going to play New York the next day and I was supposed to come off the disabled list after that weekend, which seemed to me like forever and a day.

"Listen," I said, "I think I'm going to be all right sooner."

Dave just shrugged and chewed on that wad of his.

"Why don't I go back to Cincinnati and see the doc?" I said.

"Why not?" he said and spit—and then we both went in out of the drizzle.

Well, I did go back to Cincinnati and the team doctor and he had me at the hospital, hitting the wall with a bat, which must have shook the hospital authorities but that's the way Dr. George Ballou is. He's the greatest. So is Dr. Wally Timperland, his associate. They made me a sponge guard for my hand and off I went to New York to catch up with the team. I hadn't had batting practice for eighteen or twenty days but I got to the ball park and I said, "Dave, I think I'm ready to play." Don Cardwell, who had been pitching in the majors for a dozen years, was pitching that day and he was hot. I was 0 for 4, but on the other hand I did nail two balls smack on the nose. My hand hurt, but only just a little. The next day I got 2 for 4. And then we moved down to Philadelphia, where I was coming back into form, getting 6 for 16. Yeah, that Dr. Ballou is really something. So is Dr. Timperman, his associate. They're not orthopedic doctors, a fact which discourages some of the players, but they are surgeons. Pitchers dig orthopedic doctors because guys like that are good with muscles and bones, I guess, but Dr. Ballou has been with the game a long time. Yeah, both those guys have real class.

I'm glad they're on tap each year because being in training for baseball is the toughest thing in the world. It's not like the way professional football is. If I pull a muscle on Monday I can't sit around and read the funny papers till next Sunday. I have to play the very next day. And a pulled muscle *has* to heal if you're going to play each day. I guess that's why a lot of people think us baseball players are fragile, complaining about this or that all the time, but it isn't that. Like when I had my thumb broken it was all right to bat but when my hand was in the glove the impact of a ball hitting the glove would kill me. When it gets cold my thumb still hurts. It should. I played that whole season with it swelled up like crazy.

Nineteen sixty-eight may not have been a great year for the Reds because we finished fourth, 14 games off the money, but it was sure a good year for me because that's the year I really surprised myself by batting .335. I played in 149 games, going to bat 626 times, and collected 210 hits. I hit 42 doubles, 6 triples, and 10 home runs. They walked me 56 times and struck me out 76 times. I only stole 3 bases that year compared with the 11 I had stolen in 1967, the year before. Most of the time I was out there in the outfield, playing 148 games out there to be exact. But 3 games found me back at second base. And 1 game—hang on to your hats—found me holding down first base. But that .335 of mine stuck out like my sore thumb. I led the year. I was sure proud of that and if you think I was proud, you should have seen my dad. Deron Johnson had a hot bat in 1968, too. He was fourth in the National League with .312. Tony Perez batted in the most runs for the Reds, bringing 92 guys across the plate. Alou and I were tied for the number of hits, both of us having 210 of them. Lou Brock of St. Louis beat me out in doubles. He got 46 to my 42. And when it came to doubles, Bench was right behind me in the league with 40. Beckert of Chicago scored the most runs in the National League, 98, and I was right behind him in second place because I had been lucky enough to score 94. Perez was in third place with 93 runs.

But nonetheless we ended 1968 in fourth place, which, to us, wasn't good enough.

"Wait till next year," everybody in the clubhouse kept saying, so we went home and watched Detroit beat St. Louis in the World Series, four games to three, and next year was the 1969 season, and we all know how *that* went. So as I get this book put together the 1970 season is still in front of us and hope springs eternal. Bristol is no longer with us but Sparky Anderson is and here we go again, but I am getting ahead of the story. Let's talk about batting a minute.

People are always asking about this business of a three-ball, no-strike pitch, and they're always saying, "Why do you let the next one go by when ninety-nine times out of a hundred you know it's going to be a strike and be right in there?"

Well, I hit a three-ball, no-strike pitch only once and that was for a home run. Hutch was running the team at the time and since I was in a kind of slump, he let me have a chance at it. But the odds aren't as good as you think for a good pitch coming at you. You got to tell yourself that there are certain places in the strike zone that you can clobber the ball out of sight but there are other places in the strike zone that you can't. Now if a 3 and 0 pitch is at your knees in the strike zone but not your kind of pitch, you might as well wait because you got two more pitches coming at you anyway. You've got to wait for the pitch you want more than any other pitch in the world. It's got to be right there where you like it. But some guys get too excited on a 3 and 0. They swing and miss. Listen, a strike that doesn't have your name on it is a bad pitch, no matter where it sails through the strike zone.

Anyway, being a lead-off hitter I never swing at a 3 and 0. I don't even think about it. It may be good for home-run hitters but it's not my cup of tea. Some hitters can swing at a 3 and 0 any time it strikes their fancy, but to me it's a matter of getting a good cut. The guys who wait for the right pitch are the really good cripple hitters. Sometimes that makes the difference between a one-run win and a one-run loss, which we have had more than our share of. I've made mistakes at bat and I've made mistakes out in the field, even though I am waiting out there, planning for every eventuality.

Like, there's a guy on base. Well, I got to know the score of the game, which most of us do. I got to be aware of the number of outs and who is over there on first and who is over there on second and how fast can all of these guys run and like how hard the ball might be hit. I have to know that if I go fifteen feet this way I can't throw the guy out at home and if the ball is a little flare I won't be able to throw him out at home unless he's held up a fraction of a second too long on base. I have to know how fast the batter is once he gets running. I think this is the advantage the major-league players have over the kids in Little League. We play every team about twenty times a year so we get a kind of "book" on everybody the other team has got. We even have meetings and exchange information among ourselves, like who can run fast, who has a sore arm, and who is thinking so much about buying a new car he might not have his mind 100 percent on the game. In the major leagues, you *think* baseball around the clock. There's no time off for good behavior.

If I was on another team, writing a "book" on me, I would say that Rose has a better than average arm, knows what to do with the ball when he gets it, is a good defensive outfielder, and isn't afraid to take a chance, like running into the wall. I would say Rose isn't afraid to charge to ball. I would say Rose is not afraid to have them hit over his head because he's got confidence in backtracking fast. I would say Rose is a risky outfielder, an average second baseman, but not too hot on third. Actually, I didn't like it over there at third. I went and tried my best because that's where they wanted me, but I didn't stay there over a month. On the other hand, I felt okay at second base. I tried hard to learn and master that position, but I'll be the first to admit I'm no Bill Mazeroski and I don't think I'll ever be. Right field—that's my position. Man, I'm happy in right field. I got more time to concentrate on the game out there. It's easier from the standpoint that when I was on second I had to come out to the ballpark and take fifteen minutes of ground balls a day to get the rhythm going. Listen, you play 162 games a year and you take fifteen minutes a day playing with ground balls and when July and August heat waves come, you've pooped. Maybe that's because when I went out there, I *worked* at it. Some guys just go out and loosen up. Not me. I'd work on things like making the proper throw to first and the whole bit.

Then I'd go in and change uniforms. I'd sweat that much and be that hot. The guys would kid me about it but that's okay because baseball players go around agitating each other all the time. We're born agitators, like some guys make an error and you still win the game, you tease him about it. Some of the guys get mad and some of the guys get mixed up because that's the way we agitate. Say you're agitating this guy and I'll be on your side for five minutes and just when everybody is getting so mad they don't know what to do, all of a sudden I'll switch over and start agitating the other side. I used to agitate Queen and drive him crazy. A good guy, though, but he used to get so mad. And Helms would argue with him. We'd all agitate each other. Bench is the one who can get me steamed. And I do get steamed. Nobody is safe from nobody when you get a bunch of baseball players in a bus.

There are the quiet ballplayers and there are the outspoken ones, one of which is me and I can't deny it. Now every team has a certain bunch of guys who will sit together in the back of the bus and cause grief for everybody else on the way to the ball park or to the airport. Joe Nuxhall, who pitched for the Reds when I was learning to walk and he was only fifteen himself, always managed to get the backseat by the window because I think that was a kind of superstition with him. If anybody else got his special place, he'd roust them out. And Lee May would sit back there along with me and Perez and Helms and Maloney. The quiet guys sat up front and watched the bus driver steer through traffic, but not us. We'd be in the back of the bus, agitating like crazy.

It was the same way when we flew. Usually Tommy Helms and I would sit where the stewardesses hung out for a couple of reasons and none of them are what you're thinking. One reason is, I know what everybody on the team drinks and on quick short flights I help the girls serve the drinks and the meals. So Tommy and I would go up and down the aisle, asking guys on the team things like "Coffee, tea, or me?" And that shook some of them but we were way up in the sky so there was nowhere for them to hide. The stewardesses really need help on short hops. They have to serve forty-five or fifty people fast—and before that, they usually serve about two cases of beer. It shakes some of the other passengers when we fly commercial flights. But they're good people. Lots of kidding. Then, they feel pretty good. Traveling on the same flight with a baseball team seems like an extra bonus to them. Anyway, I serve our guys to make sure they get fed because I want them to eat. Most of the time on getaway day, you don't get a lot of food. The players are hungry and I want to get them a meal. Listen, I'm more than a mother to those guys. I think that's why they never tip.

Those airlines are good and I take my hat off to all of them: Delta, United, and the rest. United does our charter flights. Bruce Walsh, the guy we've nick-named "Cloudy," works for United out of Dayton. Every time we're flying somewhere and ask him where the plane is, he looks out the window and says, "I think we're in the air." Then there's Ray Cornett out of Tampa who knocks himself out handling our reservations. A real swell guy. He calls at least once a week to ask how my dad is. Don't you think that's nice?

On those charter flights, we got a real planeload. There'll be twenty-five players all agitating one another, four coaches, the manager, sometimes Mr. Howsam, the radio and newspaper people, including Joe Nuxhall who is also agitating, guys like Ed Kennedy, Peewee Reese, Paul Campbell, and there's even more at the end of the season when they bring up the new guys. One guy I miss is Phil Seghi. He used to hold on tight and wish he was somewhere else. Phil really doesn't care much about flying and he won't take off unless he has steeled himself with a manhattan. Then he sits there the whole flight, smoking his pipe like crazy.

We've had some crazy flights, too. We were taking off one time from Houston, zooming down the runway, and we were almost at the point of no return when the pilot had to cut off because there was a big jet coming down in our path. I remember once when we circled St. Louis three hours and I don't think Mr. Seghi will ever forget that, either. Then there was the time we were flying from Milwaukee to Chicago and one of the engines caught fire—and down we had to go. Mr. Seghi will never forget that trip. But the roughest place I ever landed was in Mexico City, although the airport in Charleston, West Virginia, doesn't win any prizes. Another time, taking off from Chicago at night, we were pretty far up there in the sky and all of a sudden the emergency-exit lights flashed on. The plane zoomed back to O'Hare Field and landed—fast. They said there was a fire in one of the jets. I think after that Mr. Seghi was ready to transport all of us from Chicago to Cincinnati by taxi, but that wouldn't have looked good on the expense account.

We don't use cabs too much. Sometimes when Tommy Helms and I don't feel like hanging around the park forty-five minutes for the bus, we'll get a cab back to the hotel. Cab drivers love to talk about baseball, especially the ones who drive in New York City. On the other hand, they don't love anybody but the Mets. The cabbies in New York seem more sports-minded than the ones in San Francisco. I don't think baseball is as big there as it is in other towns. Now in Chicago there's a cab driver going around telling everybody that he's my dad. I know because another cab driver there told me, "Your dad is a cab driver with this company."

"No," I said. "My dad is a banker in Cincinnati."

"That's what you think," he said—so I let the matter drop. Cab drivers are guys I would rather not agitate.

Travel, though, is broadening, but not much when you play baseball. When I'm in Philadelphia I don't get around much to the Liberty Bell. Sometimes I'm at the 1614 Bar, where Bernie the bartender is a good guy and a baseball fan. In Chicago I'll drop in and see Gus who owns the Ink Well, where a lot of athletes hang out. Montreal? I love it. A wild town. I stay there at the Queen Elizabeth, but the ball park they have is an old park and not so hot. The park is bad, the weather is cold, but the city is great. I go to the place called George's, where the baseball players hang out. But don't get the idea I'm forever sitting in a bar. Usually, on the road, I'm up in the room, watching television.

Traveling is about the hardest work baseball has. But baseball itself is not work. And I know it doesn't look like work from the stands. Baseball looks almost too easy from up there. "How'd he miss *that* pitch?" some of the fans wonder and they mean it honestly. I couldn't believe how easy baseball did look till I watched one game once from the stands. But on the field is a different story. A ball that looks like it is coming in slow isn't. You're standing 52 feet 6 inches from the pitcher that's throwing it at you, he's throwing it up to 100 miles an hour, and you only got a split second to hit, miss, or wish you were dead.

I don't think I'd like to play—or referee—basketball full time because the fans are right there, practically on top of you. Football? Well, umpiring a game of football isn't a breeze. I think, though, the only rough call in football is the pass-interference call. If a guy holds, clips, is offside, roughs the kicker, or roughs the passer, he knows it. The only debate comes on inter-ference calls. Umpiring isn't a breeze.

The roughest call an umpire has to make in baseball is the base call, like a close play at first. Or take the trapped ball. Listen, that can fool anybody, even the guy catching it. I trapped a ball once on a televised Game of the Week. When I dove for it and spun over, there was no way on earth the umpire could see because I had blocked it with my body. And even I thought I'd caught it. I still think I caught it to this day, if that helps. But Peewee Reese said that on the instant replay it showed that I had trapped it. But listen, when it comes to umpires, I never try to put anything over on those guys in blue. The best umpire, on the other hand, can be wrong and it really takes guts for an umpire to come right out and say, "Well, I blew that one." Anyway, what are you going to say to umpires that make mistakes? Listen, I made four errors last year. Umpires are human, too, and are capable of making errors. Only it's hard to win an argument with an umpire. I pass that along for what it is worth.

Most umpires will let you get off your beef, like yell a little, but they don't want you yelling at them the rest of the game because that gets on their nerves.

Guys *have* won arguments with umpires, though. Consider the half swing. We have a rule now which says if the guy takes a half swing that the coach thinks is a strike, the manager can come out on the field and talk about it. That means the umpire down at first enters the discussion. Sometimes the call *is* reversed. But the first-base umpire can't reverse the plate umpire unless the plate umpire asks for assistance. Still, you'll see this happen lots of times: a plate umpire will call the pitch a ball and he'll look down at the first-base umpire, who will give a little sign, and the plate umpire will change the ball to a strike, which makes the batter sad but that's the way the game goes. The first-base umpire can see, which the plate umpire can't, if the batter swung. The plate umpire's view is blocked by the batter and the catcher.

But for a close call out there on the bases, you might as well forget about getting the umpire to change his mind *unless* the play involved an angle where another umpire could see it better. Still, if the guy dropped the ball in midair and the umpire didn't see it, or if he trapped the ball, you can bet your bottom dollar the umpire will reverse the call. Generally, though, umpires don't like to go around reversing the decisions of other umpires because this causes nothing but trouble and umpires don't like trouble.

They're nice guys, really, but we're not supposed to send them valentines because umpires and ballplayers are not supposed to become buddies. The fans wouldn't like that. Neither would some of the players. But we're all the time talking to each other, only most people don't know it. I remember one time during a game umpire Tony Benson was discussing with me the merits of a car he was thinking about buying. Still, we're both paying attention to our jobs. Listen, umpires have got families just like people and they like to talk. Some of them don't like to go out there and just *stand.* I'm always talking to one of them that is single, asking him about the girl situation and things of that nature.

And we *help* umpires. Like, when I was playing second base and we were setting up a play to nail the runner who was occupying my base, I'd whisper to the umpire that I had a play coming and I would appreciate if he would sort of look in. The worst thing in the world is to pick off a player and have the umpire not see it. And since those things happen fast, I like to have the umpire in on the action. I tell the guy, "Lis-

ten, be alive, will you? I'm going to pick this guy off."
So the umpire is watching and ready to call the play.

But there are some players that don't like umpires
and there are some umpires that don't like players.
That will always be the case. Umpires like that I
would never consider sending valentines to, which I
don't send to umpires anyway. And there are times I
don't feel gabby. Like, if I have an upset stomach. But
usually, out there on the field, I'm talking all the time
to umpires, other players, and if nobody wants in the
conversation, I'll talk with myself. I always talk to the
umpire at home plate when I'm batting. I remember
once that Jerry Grote, the catcher, was arguing with
the plate umpire about the pitches and they wouldn't
stop and so finally I said, "Do you guys mind not arguing so much? I'm trying to hit the ball. It's hard to
concentrate." So they both started arguing with me
all the time I was at bat and frankly, it wasn't the best
day I ever had.

I'd like to associate more with umpires but it's not
in the cards, I guess. They're really nice guys. Still, I
can't associate with them. It would look bad. They
sure lead lonely lives. They got a tough life. They
travel all the time and the only break they get is
maybe during an All-Star game. But face it. Umpires
are a big part of baseball. Without them, there
wouldn't be any game at all.

The umpiring in Little League or Knot Hole, which
I was in? Well, my favorite was a guy named Mr.
Wilson. There was another one we called Butterfly.
They were trying to do a good job and most of them
did. My dad used to tell me never to give them a hard
time because they weren't making any money out
there and that they were responsible for keeping the
games going. I give guys like that all the credit I can.

It's tough any time to officiate any game. As long as I can play baseball I don't think I'd ever want to be an umpire, though a lot of umpires were once real good ballplayers. On second thought, I don't think I'd care to be an umpire under any conditions.

When I'm playing I don't play one umpire differently than I'd do another one. I'm aware of each one of them but when I'm batting or sliding or running my fool head off, it doesn't matter to me *who* the umpire is. The only thing I feel good about is that he is there.

One time Johnny Bench was catching and it seems like most everything the pitcher threw that day the plate umpire, who shall be nameless, called it a ball, which upset Johnny Lee Bench. Finally after a 3 and 2 pitch there was another close one, the umpire called a ball, and Johnny couldn't take it any more. He started yelling unpleasant things at the umpire.

"Bench," said the umpire, "if you say one more word I'm going to bite your head off."

Bench glared and said, "If you do, you'll have more brains in your stomach than you'll have in your head."

As for me, I'm gentle with umpires. I remember one time Doug Harvey was umpiring and he was a real dramatic umpire. When he gives you the third-strike call he goes through ten thousand little poses and then bellows for all the world to hear that the call was a strike. Well, he was just starting through the first of his many poses and about to bellow when I said, "Please don't do that so loud. Listen, my mother is in the stands." He stopped in the middle of a gesture and just laughed. I was sure glad of that.

Then there is the umpire who sings to me—or rather, he used to when my post was at second base. That was Jocko Conlan. He would stand out there, looking stern and stiff, and all the while he would be singing some song called "How Many Stars in the Sky" or something like that. I will not say whether he sang good or bad. I'm not about to start any arguments with anybody about anything. But there is something about an umpire crooning to you that mellows you, doesn't it? Not much, but enough. No umpire ever sang pretty at Leo Durocher. Look at it that way, music lovers.

For the real singing, there are the Rosie Reds, the nicest bunch of ladies ever assembled. Then, there are those Barney Rapp tours. My mother goes on them. And when they travel to different parks on one of those wonderful tours they really have a ball. Barney Rapp organizes the best baseball tours anybody ever concocted. The tour guests go everywhere, do everything, and see everything, from the Sunken Gardens in Florida to ball games. It's good to be in a park away from home and hear a bunch of hometown rooters cheering us on. And there are those people who have moved from Cincinnati but still favor the Reds. In Los Angeles there's an old couple, I wish I knew their names, but they're always out there, wearing Cincinnati Reds' baseball caps, having a wonderful time, rooting for us. They're always right in the front row on the first-base side. I watch for them every time we play in Los Angeles. When you're playing games away, you expect the other team to get most of the encouragement and it gives you a good feeling, having *somebody* out there, cheering for you.

Anyway, one way or the other, the 1969 season was got through. The 1969 season was a kind of unusual season for me because I felt good all season, which means, I suppose, I talked a blue streak from the first game to the last. I did get off to a slow start, though.

The first couple of weeks we were out there in San Diego and other places and I was 3 for 19. The reason for the slow start was I didn't know the pitchers. But then I started hitting and I kept on hitting all year. You can't imagine how good I felt inside when I made that bunt the last game of the season in Atlanta. That bunt wrapped up the batting championship for me. And there I stood, looking up at the scoreboard, and that scoreboard was the most beautiful thing I think I ever saw. They made me come out of the dugout and I nodded to the people there because the scoreboard told the story. Listen, that was a real good feeling. But as for the team—well, there was pitching but there was good solid pitching on every team in the National League. I was probably the only guy in the league that got hits off every team. It's the way one guy said, "The guy that is going to hit .300 is going to hit .300 and on the other hand, the guys that ain't, ain't."

But I'll never catch up with Joe DiMaggio or those others back there in the past. That was a different day and age. Ted Williams, I think, will be the last guy to hit .400 (in 1952 he hit .400 and in 1953 he hit .407). Joe DiMaggio hit in 56 straight games. What's the hardest thing to do, hit .400 or in 56 straight games? Neither one is easy. You have to have lots of ability to do both, lots of ability and a little bit of luck.

So I just keep hustling. And hustling. And hustling. And that, to me, is the name of the game.

11 A lot of seasons have come and gone since I was a kid when my dad used to take me down to Crosley Field every chance he could beg, borrow, or steal—no, he never really stole—to get me there. The first game I ever saw there was the Dodgers. That was in the 1950s when the Dodgers had Gil Hodges, batting .283, at first base. They had Duke Snider out there in center field; he was batting in the .300s. They had Peewee Reese at shortstop. And they had Carl Erskine and Preacher Roe—from Ashflat, Arkansas—on the mound. That was when the Reds had Ted Kluszewski on first, Grady Hatton on third, and guys like Stallcup, Ryan, Wyrostek, Merriman, Usher, and Adcock. They had pitchers like Ewell Blackwell (they called him "The Whip"), Ken Raffensberger, Cincinnati native Herm Wehmeier, Howie Fox, Frank Smith, and Willie "The Knuck" Ramsdell. Incidentally, Frank Smith is one of the forty-one pitchers named Smith who have played in the major leagues. Some of the other Smiths were BroadwayAleck Smith, who played in 1901; Columbia George Smith, who played between 1916 and 1923; Germany Smith, who only played one year (1884) with Cleveland; Phenomenal Smith, who played from 1884 to 1891; Pop Smith, who played in 1883; and last but not least there was Riverboat Smith—Robert

Walkup Smith—who divided 1958 and 1959 between Boston and Cleveland. As for us Roses, there was a Chuck Rose (Charles Alfred Rose) from Macon, Montana, who pitched one year for St. Louis, the year being 1909 when he won one and lost two. Other than Chuck, I'm the only other Rose—at the moment—in the majors and some of the guys say that's even one rose too much, but that's the way guys are.

The early days of baseball seemed to have brought out the crazy names, more so than today. There was Goat Anderson in 1907, Sweatbreads Bailey in the twenties, Lady Baldwin in the 1880s, Sheriff Blake, Foghorn Bradley, Buttons Briggs, Boardwalk Brown, Three Finger Brown, Oyster Burns, Sugar Cain, Soup Campbell, Boileryard Clark, Creepy Crespi, One Arm Daily, Daisy Davis, Buttercup Dickerson, Whammy Douglas, Bones Ely, and Fat Freddie Fitzsimmons— and listen, I could go on forever. Also, add to the broadcasters' confusion Felipe, Jay, and Matty Alou— all from the Dominican Republic where nineteen of our major league players and managers first saw the light of day. Canada accounts for 117 players and managers in the majors, Cuba brought us 114, 32 came from Ireland, 31 from Puerto Rico, 28 from the United Kingdom, but we've only had one from China and one from the Canary Islands. Where are most baseball players and managers born in this country? Most came from Pennsylvania (1,142) with New York (867) second, Illinois (736) third, and Ohio (731) fourth. According to the records no National or American League manager or player was born in Hawaii or Alaska, in Nevada or Wyoming. But on the other hand, little Rhode Island got us 56 players and managers. To keep the record straight, we have no birth record of 345 players and managers. Nobody can figure out *where* they were born, so some of the stuff some of the fans might have called them might very well be true. I hope not, though.

Anyway, as I was saying, my dad used to take me to the ball park when grandstand seats, behind the painted red line, cost seventy-five cents. Every once in a while my dad would get two tickets for the Fifth-Third Bank box—he works at the bank—and that for me was the greatest. The box was right behind the dugout and the chance of collecting a foul ball was pretty good there. We always left just before the game was over to avoid the traffic. My mother used to drive up, listen to the last few innings of the game on the radio, and pick us up a few blocks from the park. Yeah, those were the good old days, but the ones now aren't so bad, either.

Even now I sometimes drop in on Bold Face Park when the boys are practicing. I'll take off my shirt and start hitting a few. *That* really brings the memories back.

Also, there is basketball now. Between baseball seasons we have a wild make-up team that plays basketball with just about anyone. With me on the team are Jim Stewart, Jim Maloney, Gerry Arrigo, Dick Vories, Skip Weber, and John Bench.

But there's a lot of stuff I haven't covered in this book and here we are, in the last chapter. Like, I've never said anything about how I met my wife. Well, her name is Karolyn, she's a doll, and she looks like a million dollars in a miniskirt. In fact, she was wearing a minidress the day I met her. There I was at the race track with a couple of other ballplayers and I had the binoculars and we were watching the race. It was at River Downs. I was calling the race for the guys. Well, I looked down along the rail and there was this girl standing real pretty, she had this minidress on, and the next thing I know, the other guys were saying, "Pete, which horse is winning?"

"Don't bother me right now," I said. And meant it because right then I had lost all interest in horses.

I found a guy I knew who knew her, he told me who she was, so I called her the next day, and we went out together. At first she wasn't sure who I was. The name Pete Rose rang a kind of bell, though.

"Oh," she said on the telephone that day, "you're a football player or something. Is that it?"

"I used to be," I said.

And seven months later we were married. She's the greatest. She's got real class. She gets along great with the wives of the other players, she's a good swimmer, and she can throw a baseball pretty good. Her father—Fred Engelhardt—is a carpenter at Mabley & Carew, the department store here, and he's got the master's touch when it comes to woodwork. He's made me a bar. He's made me a case for my souvenir bats. And once, as a swimmer in the state championship, he competed against Johnny Weissmuller, the first movie Tarzan that I can remember. He has been wonderful to me and so has his wife. My wife's grandmother used to be in show business, playing the stage here in Cincinnati when they had good stage shows. My mother-in-law is Pearl—and she *is* a pearl! She loves baseball. She goes to every game she can and she's personality plus. She's my wake-up gal. Whenever I have to be out of the sack early, she calls, so I don't have to set my alarm. Because I'm on the road so much and Karolyn travels with me a lot, my mother-in-law has practically raised my little girl. But when I first started going with their daughter, they took a dim view of guys like me.

What I mean is, they were strict with their daughter in the nicest old-fashioned ways. They wouldn't let her stay out late, not even on New Year's Eve. If they were shocked because their pretty daughter had fallen in love with a ballplayer, I couldn't tell. I was too impressed—and too much in love with Karolyn—to notice things like that, if the things existed. I had Karolyn and I had baseball and I had my Grand Prix, the finest set of wheels I'd owned. What more could a growing boy want?

And now there is my daughter, Fawn (she calls herself Pete Rose the Second), and my son, who is really Pete Rose the Second but because of my daughter we call him Junior.

Pearl, my mother-in-law, is one of those wonderful ladies who always has a whopping old-fashioned dinner and a huge birthday cake whenever anybody's birthday rolls around. And she always fixes me chicken and dumplings—hers are the best ever created—after a game. On the other hand my own mother, before the game, will fix me scrambled eggs because she feels if she does that I'll get three hits. It's a wonder I don't weigh a ton. But maybe I won't. My dad is always trotting around and so am I. Still, I'll never be the guy my dad is. He's quite a guy. Maybe it's old-fashioned these days to say things like that, but they need to be said—at least as far as I'm concerned. He never changes. If I can have my way, I want to be the same person, whether I make a million a year or a few thousand bucks. I never want to get a big head. I want to be nice to people because a lot of people—more than I deserved—have been nice to me. Oh, there will always be some people who *aren't* nice, but that's something we all have to live with, isn't it? It's those nice people I'm thinking about here.

I'm thinking of guys like Hy Ullner, who is just

about the nicest guy ever to come down the pike. One day a guy asked me what I was doing with my money. When I said I was just socking it away in a bank, they introduced me to Hy Ullner and the first thing I knew he started me putting money in different investments. He doesn't get a dime out of it. He's made his million, nobody gave it to him, he went out and earned it himself. I have a lot of faith in him. I can trust him. Even if he lost all my money I would still trust him. He's not my manager. He's like an investment counselor who gets a kick out of helping ballplayers. He gets no percentage. Now he's taking care of Johnny Bench, too. Then there's Ann Smith and Jack Meyers at Professionals, Incorporated. Ann is a sharp dealer. And Jack is, too. With people like Hy Ullner, Ann Smith, and Jack Meyers looking out for me, I got more time to concentrate on baseball, which I should be doing anyway.

People are always asking if I ever meet any Hollywood celebrities. My mother is always asking, so is my dad, so I'll mention a few here. Like Milton Berle has been a good friend of mine. He comes to all the games he can. And he's always teasing me. He comes to the clubhouse and joking like there is no tomorrow. He's great. Then there's Max Baer, Jr., who is in the "Beverly Hillbillies." We were out with him one night in Hollywood at a place called the Daisy Club and all he talked about was sports because that's what he really ached to be a part of. We ran into Bobby Darrin there that night and even Steve Allen came by and said hello. The funniest thing there, though, was Don Adams, who plays on "Get Smart." Well, there Don Adams is, watching "Get Smart" on the tube and he's telling this gal he's with everything that's going to happen next. I had wanted to see a game on the tube, but Don Adams wouldn't let me change channels. He just sat there with this chick, telling her, "Now watch this guy sneak up behind me and now watch me go off the roof. . . ."

Met Doris Day in Hollywood. Met Hugh O'Brian, who was Wyatt Earp. Met Chuck Connors. Then there is Joy Colton, who used to live in Ohio—Columbus, to be exact—only she lives out on the Coast now, she comes to all the games, and is a real good kid. The other day she went out to Disneyland and got a Mickey Mouse watch for my little daughter. She's got her own travel agency in California and she's a good friend of all the Dodgers. So all the people in Hollywood aren't stars, but all the ones I've met—the stars and the others—all turned out to be real nice. So, if you're looking for some inside scoop on who is divorcing whom, you'll have to look elsewhere.

Kids are the greatest fans. I love them. I like the ones who come around and throw questions at me, like how do I feel about a sacrifice bunt? I tell them it's just like what it sounds like, a *sacrifice* bunt. And I tell them it helps the team win and anything that helps the team win is okay by me. And the kids are always asking, "How can I improve at bunting?"

Well, practice makes perfect. That's what I tell them and the advice I'd pass along to any kid. If you bunt bad in practice, you bunt bad in the game. The thing is to just try to bunt strikes because a ball that's out of the strike zone isn't the easiest to bunt. Don't try to push the ball, I tell them, just try to meet it. Relax. Don't get a death grip on your bat. Don't move your bat towards the ball. Stay loose. Your arms should be loose and your back should be loose. Be as loose as Ted Williams and you got it made.

"Did you ever catch in the majors?" one guy asked me once.

Sure, but only in practice. Once, though, I almost caught in the All-Star Game. This was out in California in 1967. I didn't get to play till the fourteenth inning in what was the longest All-Star Game in history. Perez ended the game in the fifteenth inning with a homer to let the National League win 2 to 1. Thirty batters were struck out in that game. The American League didn't allow a single walk. Anyway, they put me in as a pinch hitter and I popped up and that was that. I had made the team as the fourth outfielder but since I was the only one with catching experience left Walter Alston kept me on the bench in case he needed a catcher. I'll never forget that day. Walter looked up and down the bench and said, "Can anybody here catch?"

"I can," I said.

You should have seen Bristol's face when he heard I was sitting around, waiting to catch. But it never happened. I was the only catcher they hadn't used but they ended up putting me on second.

Frankly, I wouldn't mind catching in the majors. Who knows? I may get the chance yet! It's fun to look into the future, isn't it? Like, looking ahead to the 1970 season which, by the time this book comes out, will have just started. I figure it's going to be a good season for us. I hope it's going to be a good season for me as far as records go. Look at the 1970 this way. We'll be moving into that beautiful new stadium. I'm captain of the team. We've got a new manager. And I've reached a kind of plateau, making $100,000 to play the game. Looking over the others, I'd say that Houston has a real good club, but on the other hand, all the clubs in our division are pretty hot. Every club in our division has its share of good pitchers. The Braves helped themselves with Jim Hunter. The Dodgers have good pitching, so have the Giants, and so has San

Diego. This is going to be a pretty evenly matched
league, but I think the Reds have the best offense.
Now let's all cross our fingers and hope the right people stay healthy, get off to a good start, make their
own breaks, and don't get off in the season with a 2
and 12 or something. Listen, you can lose the whole
darned season in that first month. We just have to
play hard every day. There's no time off for good
behavior. We got to grab the momentum and never let
loose. The Mets proved that last year. They had
momentum that wouldn't quit. They had it there in
the first game of the play-off with the Braves and they
never let go of it till they wrapped up the World Series. I dig those Mets. They've got a tremendously
strong pitching team and they had a guy like Frank
Robinson, who—in my opinion—woke the Mets up
last year. You know, the Orioles beat them the first
game of the series and Frank Robinson said they
looked like a bunch of corpses over there, sleeping, so
they came back strong the next day. Frank must sure
have said the right words to make them aware of
what was going on. He's just naturally great, isn't he?
Maybe the first game of the Series they were too busy
looking to be playing. It's like when we played the
Astrodome for the first time, there stood Dave Bristol,
chewing that wad, and giving us looks.

"This will be the first time you play here," he said.
"So all of you get your tails out there early and gawk.
Get the sight-seeing out of your system because you
got no time for it when the game starts."

That made sense and still makes sense, doesn't it?
When you're playing baseball, you're playing baseball
—*period*. That's why I'm not one of these "business"
ballplayers. I'm business-minded in the winter but
once the season starts, I don't go down to the stock

markets and look at the boards or anything like that. After all, look at it this way. Every business I'm connected with depends on how I play baseball. That's why, when the season is on, I don't have time to think about anything but baseball. I have to think baseball 115 percent of the time. Like we have a basketball player right now as I write this, he's going into bankruptcy, he's being sued, and everything. Can he be out there performing his best? That's why a lot of owners don't like their players to go into business because thinking about business—instead of the sport—might mess them up. I guess I'm what you might call a *dedicated* baseball player. I know the other businesses I have aren't going to produce if I don't produce out there on the field.

I'm dedicated and I'm a company man. You take Sparky Anderson, the forty-fourth manager the Reds had since they got in the National League for keeps eighty-five years ago. Frankly, I've never played for him. All he knows about me is what he has seen and what he has heard. The fact he has enough faith in me to make me the team captain means, you might say, that means he's putting his job in my hands. Well, I'm going to try to do the best I can for him. This doesn't mean I don't like Dave Bristol or the others. It means only that I'm in a kind of business, which is what baseball is. Get married to only one manager? Not on your life. In baseball everybody knows there are certain times, whether you agree or not, that personnel is going to change. If you're a player you got to believe that what is happening is for the best, otherwise you're no good during the season. Listen, I probably liked Dave Bristol more than any manager I've ever had but that's not saying I don't like the others, does it? Just because one guy gets the ax doesn't mean the next guy is a dog. The way I feel, when a new manager shows up, I'm going out of my way to make him like me. I want Sparky Anderson to be proud that *I'm* taking the lineup card out there. I want to be proud to say that I play for Sparky. That's the way baseball should be. Sometimes, though, with some players it isn't, but I can't speak for them. I can only speak for myself.

Listen, I can't even speak for the fans. When the game is on, they're one place and I'm another. If they boo me I feel bad but I don't bawl. Some fans will boo you whether you're good or bad. All I know is, you get 30,000 fans in the stands you feel good. When you play to only 7,000, voices carry more because of the emptiness, and you can hear people calling you a bum. But you always get fans who ride you because that's baseball. You take it because you make good money. But when I strike out, I got news for you. I feel worse than any of the fans. If I don't do good, it comes out of my salary. It doesn't come out of the fan's pocket. But you know what I try to do if a fan gives me a hard time? I try to get to a baseball and toss it—real nice—up to where he is. That'll either make him like me or it will embarrass the heck out of him. And I'm not trying to bribe the guy. It's just my way of doing, doing something nice for him, like getting him a ball or an autograph. I mean, why get mad and yell back? People pay to enjoy you play. They don't come to be bad-mouthed by some guy in a baseball uniform.

As for autographs, I don't sign them because a guy is supposed to. I sign them because I get a big kick out of it and I *want* to do it. It's the same reason I hustle. I hustle because I get a kick out of playing baseball, it's easy and it comes natural, and if it was hard work —and no fun—I'd want to get out of it because the way

I feel is, nobody should work at anything that is hard and no fun. So now and then I'll have a bad day, so what? I figure I'm going to have more good days than bad ones. If I play a game so I can go to the mirror and tell myself I did the best I actually could and the best I know how—and if I can do that and keep a straight face—then I feel like I'm kidding myself. It's like I could have done better. Listen, I chew myself out more than any manager ever will. As for fans chewing me out, no sweat. I've had days where I've gone 4 for 4—four real solid hits—only then I'll come to bat with one run down, a guy on second, and get a strike, and they'll boo me. That's the way some fans are. But I firmly believe that if a guy pays three or four bucks to see you play he can do anything he wants so long as he doesn't throw out something that will hit and hurt you. But he can yell till he's blue in the face. I don't care. It breaks the monotony, which is a lot more than I do a lot of times.

"Do the kids today have the same chance you had?"

They ask me that and I look over the Little League scene and the Knot Hole scene and I'm afraid I have to say no. Things have changed, haven't they? Like, they can't practice as much as I used to. It's tough to get a field. Forty thousands kids around here play baseball, each team has to really struggle to get to use a field, and the old story is that the team that usually wins is the one that practices three or four times a week. Also, kids don't go out on their own and play baseball any more. Who plays stickball these days? Most kids don't go to practice now unless their mothers chauffeur them. I used to walk to practice or thumb, but I never allow my own kids to do that these days. There's too much bad stuff going on now, kids getting stabbed, and stuff like that. We didn't have that to worry about when we were that age. I guess times have changed and when they change, they don't always change for the better, do they?

Maybe I was just lucky. I hope I keep on being lucky. I hope I get by so I can quit at the top. When I do quit, I want to be in a business where I can go to as many baseball games as I want. I don't want to get caught in traffic jams, going to and from work. I guess my automobile business would be the best thing to concentrate on. This eight-hour-a-day stuff I don't like too much. Like, after I came back from Geneva, New York, my first time in the bushes, I worked that winter at the Cincinnati Union Terminal, loading express cars for Railway Express. My aunt Evelyn Trust got me on there. I used to load railroad cars from midnight to eight in the morning within whistling distance of Crosley Field. I used to load a whole boxcar by myself each night. It was around the Christmas season. I worked from October to the end of December and made $2.83 an hour. Listen, I was making more there than I was making playing baseball. It was okay. The guys were all good to me. We used to sneak out on coffee breaks when we weren't supposed to and I'd get off at eight, go home, sleep, and meet this girl I knew when she got out of Western Hills High School in the afternoon. Loading boxcars was okay, as I say, but when I can't play baseball any more I don't think I'd care to go back into that line of work.

Maybe I'd do some broadcasting of sports, but if I went that route, I'd want to go to college and take some lessons in speech. I figure people listening deserve somebody who knows what he's talking about. So I'd need schooling. They wouldn't want to hear me hem and haw and stutter. That's all they would hear now if I went directly into broadcasting. It's one thing to be interviewed; it's another to do the interviewing.

Actually when I can't play for the Reds any more, or even before that, I think I would like to be a playing manager. It's not much different from being a playing captain. And if somebody was better in the outfield than me, I'd yank me fast. But I'd have to have a great coaching staff to help me. I think the big part of managing is knowing your pitchers inside and out. You have to know when to take them out of the game and when to leave them in. There's good managing and there's bad managing. I wouldn't know what kind I'd be till I got in there and tried. I believe a manager is only as good as the players he has. If you don't have the horses, you can't pull the stagecoach. Would guys resent me if there were trades? I don't think, in baseball, that everybody resents being traded. Jerry Arrigo wanted to be traded. I'm pretty sure of that. When he figured he wasn't going to be allowed to pitch for the Reds he wanted to go to Chicago where he would get the chance. I'd like to see him go like a million dollars there, wouldn't you? He's got class and he deserves all the good that baseball has to offer, but the point is, not all guys resent being traded. As for me, right now, all I can do is play hard and observe.

Being team captain is a good start, I think. You learn different things, like explaining the ground rules and stuff. They never change, but then you got the job of taking the lineup card out. As team captain I don't think I'll be the buffer between Sparky and the players. If I have a complaint or if they have a complaint, we'll each go straight to Sparky. That's the way it should be. I'm a player and I'm a company man and I'm not ashamed to admit it. The company is the Cincinnati Reds and that's who I work for. If they don't want to fly us in charter planes, no sweat. I'll not rave. They're the ones that sign my check. I just hope that I can make the front-office guys—and the fans they represent—proud that I'm associated with the team. But there are some guys who will, naturally, gripe about everything. Listen, they'll gripe if they got a well-stacked brunette sitting in the plane with them, they'll gripe cause she's not a blonde. Guys will gripe in any business.

How long will my career last? I don't really know. The good Lord willing, and if the physical aspect holds up, I think I can play until 1980. I think I can keep myself in shape that long. I sure hope so. And I'd like to play the rest of my big-league career with the Cincinnati Reds. I want to be the guy who played his whole career in the majors on his hometown team and then went on to become manager of it. A lot of people say a guy shouldn't play in his own hometown. They bring up how Herm Wehmeier was booed out of Cincinnati in 1954, but I'm not sure about that kind of thing. As for me, all I can do is keep my nose clean and try to produce. If I produce well enough they won't be able to boo me. I'm going to have bad days and I'm going to have good days and, as I keep telling you, I just hope I have more good days than bad ones.

If I manage to stay here, that will be another first. I was the first to be both an All-Star infielder and All-Star outfielder. I was the first Red to win batting titles back to back. I was the first local to be made captain. I was the first Red to be a $100,000 ballplayer; so I guess I can be first to do anything—if I want it enough to work hard enough for it. Then again, if I got traded tomorrow, I would just pat Mr. Howsam on the back and have no hard feelings. He has been great to me the same as all of them—and you—have been. I'd just say that I had enjoyed my stay with the Reds because, after all, when it's all over this is where I'm coming back to live. The fans here are great. They have real class. But if I got traded tomorrow I'd still feel the same way—and I'd depart without a grumble. I'd go to the team that got me and I would prove to them they were smart to get me. If I couldn't do it, I just couldn't do it, but it wouldn't be because I didn't try. I'll do it here or anywhere—on ability. That's all I got to offer. You won't find me getting mad and yelling and moaning. I'm paid to play baseball—period.

If I were manager—whew! What would I do they don't do now? I'd let the players speak up a little more for what they want. But on the other hand, I'll be the first to admit it's not easy to keep everybody happy these days. I would try to get across to the players how much a championship team means to them. I don't mean just financially, which isn't to be sneezed at, but I mean in later years, too. I would try to get the players to see that baseball isn't a job. As for coaches, I would pick the guys who are good workers and who know baseball. I'd have Helms coaching. I think coaches should be spark plugs. Hal Smith was just great. He'd catch batting practice, he'd hit fungoes, he'd do everything and anything. Yeah, and I wouldn't hesitate to fire a guy. But it's always easy to fire a guy, isn't it? Sometimes, it's too easy. Gil Hodges was a great manager last year. He got the guys believing in themselves. It's a question of getting the team to operate as a unit. That might take a month. It might take six years. Listen, I've been here seven and it hasn't happened yet, has it? Every year I think our team is going to go like a house afire and every year it never happens. We get into a winning streak and all of a sudden there goes our momentum, flying out the window.

But each year hope springs eternal because each year we're back out there. Maybe 1970 will be the year with the magic in it. I sure hope so. Cincinnati is a good baseball town and it deserves having a real winner. I'll bet there's confetti stored away on the top floors of our office buildings that's never even been opened or tossed out. All of Cincinnati is waiting to go wild and so am I and so is the rest of the team and so is Mr. Howsam and so is—well, you know what I mean. The last time it happened to us was 1961. And before that, you have to go clear back to 1940 and 1939 to know what it feels like to have a winner. And before that you have to go clear back to 1919.

Listen, I think we've all waited long enough. I think it's time we got the show on the road. All I know is, we're sure going to try to make it happen, which is all any guy can promise.

So I guess the book is over and I'm sorry that it isn't better than it is but we got to face facts, like I'm more comfortable in right field than I am putting a book together. I suppose I should end this book with some brilliant advice to the world, but I've got no brilliant advice to give because I've still got a lot of growing up to do myself. All I know is they go around saying, "It's not whether you win or lose but how you play the game." My dad never believed that and neither do I. Winning is what counts and don't you ever forget it. What I mean is, it doesn't matter what you're trying to do—play Little League, be a good father, put in a day's work for a day's pay, raise your kids so they grow up right, or get the right girl to marry you—they don't pay you to lose.